To Dad,
From Kelly

TO DAD,
FROM KELLY

A memoir about fathers and sons, lessons
and questions, life and death

Kelly Lytle

ISBN: 0692250387
ISBN 13: 9780692250389
Library of Congress Control Number: 2014912209
Kelly Lytle, Cleveland, OH

For Mom and Erin
"Life is like a box of chocolates.
Every day is a big bite."
Rob Lytle

AUTHOR'S NOTE

Drafts of "Catch," "Lytle Would Play," "Walk Before You Run," and "Ain't Time to Quit" have appeared on my blog at www.kellylytle.com. I have changed some names to protect the innocent.

James Brunner designed and created the cover art for *To Dad, From Kelly*. James is a graphic designer and illustrator in the San Francisco area. We grew up in Fremont, Ohio, together and have known each other for nearly two decades. I am honored that James worked with me on this project. His immense talents are on display at www.manovermars.com.

To Dad, From Kelly

PREFACE

This is a book about fathers and sons, life and death, and the celebration of life in death. It is a book about my father and about me.

I was born on September 12, 1982. That morning, Dad looked at my mom and said, "Please, Tracy, you've got to be kidding me. Not today." It was opening day of the 1982 National Football League (NFL) season. Dad, a backup running back for the Denver Broncos, had a game that afternoon versus the San Diego Chargers. He also had a pregnant wife who was about to give birth to me with barely enough time for a police escort to lead him from the hospital to Denver's Mile High Stadium for the opening kickoff. The Broncos lost the game, and the next day a cartoon in a local newspaper mocked the timing of my delivery. Dad and I were close from the start.

I believe that every life has defining moments, experiences that singe our psyches. Time froze for me on November 20, 2010, when a doctor entered a small waiting room near the lobby of Memorial Hospital in Fremont, Ohio. His pained face still haunts me. I see it when I remember how the words "I'm sorry" floated in slow motion from his mouth. Dad had died of a heart attack at 56. Death had detonated family life for my mom, my sister Erin, and me.

Through misty eyes, I saw the doctor exit our room. Air fled my lungs. Sorrow choked me. Mom, Erin, and I collapsed into each other's arms, a tangled mess of family that had been blindsided by the impossible permanence of death. Although I cannot know how it feels to die, this moment taught me how death feels. I had idolized Dad all my life. He was invincible until he was dead.

As I've considered my upbringing, I see that there are traditional, if stereotypical, illustrations of Midwestern families. Then there is mine. Mom and Dad began dating in high school. They attended the University of Michigan together and married after graduating in 1977. Dad achieved a small measure of fame for his exploits as an All-American running back for Michigan and then for his seven seasons playing professional football with the Broncos. He finished third in the voting for the 1976 Heisman Trophy, the award given annually to college football's best player, graduated from Michigan as the school's leader in career rushing yards, and scored Denver's lone touchdown in their Super Bowl XII loss to the Dallas Cowboys.

Erin was born in 1980. I followed in 1982. Our family moved from Denver to my parents' small, Northwest Ohio hometown of Fremont after Dad retired from football in 1984. We ate dinner together as a family every night, had dogs, a yard, and a fence. Laughter from family and friends filled our home. My family could fit somewhere inside the idealized vision of a quaint American household, only life is never that easy.

Dad's death hurt like nothing I had ever experienced. Agony and regret became close friends of mine. I constructed a façade of stoicism, but my tears outsmarted me. I cried driving in my car, while watching Michigan football games, and one night while slumped against a brick wall outside a musty bar where I had downed too many beers. When the tears wanted to strike, they held me at their mercy.

A year after Dad died, a friend encouraged me to write him a letter. I resisted, trembling at the thought of confronting the loss I wanted to bury. The friend persisted, though, and after many conversations, I relented. I wrote Dad a letter. A second one followed. Then I wrote several more letters that I had nowhere to send but knew I needed to write. Emotions poured from my heart and flooded my head. Writing these feelings started my healing. They inspired this book.

The more I wrote, the more I felt my grief subside. I woke to write before the sun rose most days and embraced late evenings when pen, paper, and bittersweet loneliness accompanied me through memories both pleasant and painful. Telling these stories started as a mechanism for healing but became something more important. Through the lens of my relationship with my dad, I faced my life with honest eyes for the first time. I considered the lessons

I learned from Dad while confronting the questions of him I never had had the guts to ask. I confessed my deepest fears over failing to match his legacy. I reflected on the person I wanted to be thanks to the values he taught.

Dad was a man who placed others above himself. He embraced people. He taught inclusion over exclusion and inspired others to believe more in themselves. I watched him walk into crowds of strangers and leave to the laughter of new friends. He deflected talk of his accomplishments because modesty mattered more to him than any achievement. Not a day passes that I don't rely on something I learned from him.

This book is my attempt to remember the father who shaped me through his unique blend of humor, kindness, and self-deprecation. Dad lived somewhere between the innocent and the instigator. To me, he was a father, friend, mentor, and teacher. And he played these roles with a playful, often devious smile spread across his face.

My stories are as authentic as time allows. Too many years have passed for every conversation to be perfect, but the context, emotions, and personal significance are all honest. As with most memories, the truth exists somewhere between what is real, what I remember, and what nostalgia has embellished. The pages to follow are the lessons I learned from Dad and the questions that I wish we either answered or asked. They are personal reflections whose messages I hope resonate with others.

Dad always said, "It ain't about what's done; it's about what you do with what's done that counts." His premature death is done. Sharing what he meant as a father is my choice to do something that counts.

WHEN YOUR HERO FALLS

I gave a tribute to Dad at his memorial service on the morning of November 24, 2010. The secret I have kept hidden until now is that I wrote that speech on a Friday evening in October 2008. On that night, Dad made a passing confession about his health, one that I feared counted for life and death. A simple sentence made me realize that my once invincible father was not simply beatable, but beaten. I knew my dad was dying two years before he died.

In 2001, I left Ohio for Princeton University. After graduating from Princeton in 2005, I lived in New York City for three years before returning to Ohio in mid-2008 to work as a sparsely paid intern in the salary cap office for the Cleveland Browns professional football team. Although I had visited home for summer stretches and holidays during my seven years away, I had spent most of that time bouncing between friends and local bars. I had people to see and parties to attend. When I did stick around our house, I spent more time on my phone connecting with friends from school or Manhattan. I blew through these weekends at home as a mindless whirlwind that never slowed down to appreciate anything, including Dad's health. Since I can remember, I had equated Dad with Superman. He was unbeatable when I left for college, and I assumed this would never change. I assumed wrong.

Dad's condition shocked me when I moved back to Ohio. Now living in Cleveland, about ninety miles from my parents in Fremont, I saw Dad more often and observed his health in more detail. His presence felt older, and not because his hair had thinned and caught a hint of gray. He trudged more slowly than I remembered. His pained face revealed more of the hurt blitzing his body from years of surgeries and violent collisions endured during his NFL career. Dad's mood seemed somber and his spirit resigned. He lacked the fight he once had. The subtle changes made him different from the man I remembered.

In October 2008, the Browns had their bye weekend for that NFL season, and the rare reprieve from my job allowed me to spend a weekend at home with Mom and Dad. On Friday night, Dad and I traveled forty miles southwest to Findlay, Ohio, to watch a high school football game. We drove a curved path cut by a two-lane country road that wound through the small towns where we each had competed in sports as kids. At first, Dad and I talked about the financial crisis then choking the American economy. I confessed to losing $1,000 betting on the survival of Lehman Brothers, once one of Wall Street's most iconic banks. Dad reminded me that my small misstep paled when pitted against his losses over the years. Men of money we are not, we both agreed.

With almost one hour of uninterrupted time together, it was only a matter of time before our attention turned to the sporting events that defined so much of our shared past. Soon, our conversation became one about old track meets and football games, about great plays made and missed. Our destination, Findlay, held a special place in our hearts. Findlay is one of Fremont's main sports rivals, and Dad recalled running over, around, and through their high school team many years before in another of his All-American high school gridiron performances for Fremont. I saw Findlay as the town where I clanged two free throws off the rim and lost a fifth-grade basketball tournament for my team in the final seconds of a one-point loss.

"Man, I still remember that choke job you had here," Dad teased as we rolled along a street lined with fast food signs and an old video rental store. "You remember it?"

"Of course I do. It still pisses me off."

"Ha," Dad said.

"What are you giving me grief about? It's not like you could have made them." We laughed, savoring the slice of the finest Midwest nostalgia our memories could serve.

Dad and I found a place to stand on the sidelines during the game, keeping our distance from the players and coaches. The sun's descent marked the close of another fall day as the stadium roared to life. Leaves made a bouquet of burnt orange, faded yellow, red, and brown in the trees surrounding us. Towering lights lit the field so that everyone, even Dad and I, grasped a hint of the spotlight. The air's touch turned brisk, and a rising wind swept against our faces.

We spoke little, reserving our comments for impressive plays. Mostly, we watched. And we listened. Cheers bounced from one side of the stadium to the other. Cheerleaders shrieked annoying shrills of encouragement that nobody heard. Coaches screamed for more effort, more speed, more anything, more everything. Shoulder pads thumped at every collision. Excitement struck the sidelines with each important play. I don't remember the game's final score, but at 26 years old, my time spent with Dad helped me remember what it felt like to be a kid. I enjoyed every second.

As the game approached its end, Dad and I left the stadium and walked to his car. We began our trek home. Unlike our earlier talk, though, our conversation turned more serious.

"Kelly, I'm tired all the time," Dad said, admitting for the first time that fatigue was overtaking his body much like the October darkness enveloping the empty road we traveled. "But I know I'll come around. I can tough it out."

"I know you will Dad. Just give it some time," was my only reply.

We both stared into the blackness ahead and talked little for the remainder of the trip. My recent fears crystallized in that instant. Dad was suffering more than I had realized. He had built his professional football career on persevering against injuries. He used numbing injections to hobble through practices. He concealed his pain with blended humor and sarcasm. To reach the professional ranks required that Dad sacrifice himself without regard for the future. Although I often boasted of his toughness, the truth was that I understood a mere fraction of the trauma he bore.

Scars zigzagged everywhere on his arms and legs. Dad's bloated knees challenged his walking with each painful step. His rusty joints needed the grease of painkillers to function. These visible, physical wounds were the ones everyone saw. What I didn't know, and what scared me more than anything in my life, was the glimpse Dad had offered into his internal misery.

From Dad's words, I sensed that he knew he had begun his descent on the varied but finite curve of life. Questions I knew that I should ask about his health and how I could help flooded my brain. I needed to go deeper and do something, anything, for my father, but fear stiff armed me. I retreated. My hero had just made a painful admission, and I could only shield my eyes and ears from its truth. Alone in my bedroom later that night, I wrote my father's eulogy.

This was October 2008. Dad died in November 2010. For the next twenty-five months, I stayed on the outside as other instances deepened my fears. Some were small and easy to discard, like the day in November 2008 when Dad returned to Ann Arbor, Michigan, to serve as an honorary captain for Michigan in their football game versus Northwestern. Dad and I attended the ceremony together, and as we toured Michigan's facilities, we spoke to several former players and school administrators. I watched Dad fumble through his memory to recall names and faces. His comments arrived a step late and lacked social awareness. He wasn't inappropriate, but he came close. I had never seen Dad struggle socially in this way. The moment left me confused and fearful.

Six weeks later, Dad suffered a stroke. I ignored his mental slippage at Michigan and blamed his physical deterioration on this looming near-catastrophe. The stroke shielded me from confronting the severity of Dad's decline.

Recovering in the months following his stroke, Dad returned to work and applied a veneer of normalcy to his routine. Still, though, a pattern of unusual behavior emerged. He lost track of key dates and meetings more often. Mom forced him to list all of his tasks and follow strict schedules, and she helped him set reminders for every meeting. Despite the new regimen, Dad never seemed right.

On occasion, he shied away from holding his newborn granddaughter, my sister's daughter, Audrey. Dad loved children and to see him shrink from immersing himself in their playful ways was something foreign to our family. Did Dad fear his crippled hands couldn't hold her? Through it all, I refused to admit that Dad's mind and body were failing. I certainly never spoke to him about it. The thought of doing so hurt me too much.

Dad's mood also changed during the months between his admission of being "tired all the time" and his eventual death. It didn't sour so much as turn melancholy. He questioned his purpose more than before. He wondered if his life, both inside and outside football's white lines, held any use for others. He limped through each day believing that he had failed at every turn.

A lifetime of playing football had broken Dad on the outside many years earlier. As I reflect on this time now, I see that as his death neared his heart and mind had been defeated, too.

It haunts me to admit that when I first realized my dad was dying two years before his death, I chose not to accept what I knew to be true. In the years since, I've written many stories of Dad and me. Despite the colorful images I can create of my father, the tragedy I feel over a simple drive home from a high school football game is the memory I cannot escape. I see Dad's wounded face from that night. His color appears more ghostly than alive. Eyes that roared with intense vitality for many years seem sunken, beaten down by his suffering. His grin, once a playful mix of sarcasm and feigned innocence, begs for mercy. When I close my eyes, I see this face, and I worry that it will never leave.

I wish I had said something when my hero began to fall. If I could change history, I would change this night. My heart would not stay silenced; my fears would not stay buried. I would ask questions that Dad didn't want to answer. I would force conversations that he didn't want to have. The sad reality of such talks would sting beyond imagination, but I would not run from them. My hero would still topple, of course, but at least I would be at his side as he did.

The agony of defeat, circa 1983

"LYTLE WOULD PLAY"

I always marveled at my dad's hands. If I looked hard enough, I could imagine them in their prime, one powerfully clutching a football and the other jabbing at an opponent in his path. In real life, though, I saw his hands as a gateway for suffering. His bloated and arthritic fingers pointed in ten directions. Each one carried a combat story from his days playing football.

I watched Dad labor to get through each day for almost three decades before he died. I can remember him trying to stand. He'd push himself off a couch or chair, make it halfway, and falter. His knees would wobble and silent screams would seem to wail from his eyes. He'd brace himself against a headrest or nearby table and finally stand. I'd watch, then forget. The most familiar sights are the easiest to ignore.

As Dad's life neared its end, the sport he loved had reduced this once celebrated athlete to limps and winces. But Dad never mentioned the pain; complaining wasn't part of his makeup. Besides, I don't think he felt he had any right to grumble. As a boy, he had dreamed of playing professional football, and he had realized his dream. By his own admission, he accepted the costs with a single regret: that his myriad injuries kept him from reaching his potential and forced his retirement before he was ready to say goodbye.

Now, with his life abbreviated at the age of 56, I wish I could ask Dad one more time if he still believed all the treatments, operations, excruciating mornings, prescription drug dependence, and even his early death remained the acceptable collateral damage for an athletic goal achieved. Would Dad accept the same deal he made with football's devils if he knew the real outcome?

To understand my dad one needed to recognize that his life had a singular mission. Growing up in Fremont, Dad told his parents and two sisters that he would play professional football. To him, this pronouncement wasn't a boast but a fact. He charted a course to the NFL, and he prepared himself to endure whatever abuses and sacrifices were necessary to achieve it.

In playground basketball games against older neighborhood kids, he wrapped ankle weights above his shoes, believing they would strengthen his legs enough to withstand the punishment of the career he envisioned. Later, in junior high school, he started lifting weights and running sprints with the older players on the high school's varsity team. He craved the satisfaction that came with challenging the bigger, stronger, and faster high school kids. "Couldn't get enough of it," Dad told me years later. "All I wanted was to keep practicing. Every day, hell, every minute. I loved football, Kelly."

People doubted his abilities. Find another dream, they said. You're too small, too slow, or too white ever to play in the NFL. But Dad refused to listen. "I didn't care," he said. "Nothing was stopping me. Nobody knew how hard I would work to get there. Nobody realized how much I *had* to play football."

I wonder if the same obsession would consume Dad if he knew how life would dead end. Maybe it doesn't matter. Football chose Dad as much as he chose football. He loved the sport as a parent loves a child, unconditionally.

High school, college, and NFL teammates praised Dad. Throughout my life, I heard their stories about how he persevered through injuries and dedicated his body to the team. Legendary Michigan football coach Bo Schembechler called him one of the toughest players he had ever coached, saying that Dad absorbed abuse while playing like an "ugly outsider trying desperately for the last spot on the team."[1]

---

1   Schembechler, Bo and Mitch Albom. *Bo: Life, Laughs, and Lessons of a College Football Legend*. Random House Value Publishing, 1991. Print.

Following Dad's memorial service, I heard from several former Michigan players that Coach Schembechler judged future generations of Wolverines by their willingness to pry their battered bodies from the training room table for another grueling practice. To coax players off the injured list and onto the field, the coach would often say, "Lytle would play."

After Dad's death, his teammates echoed this sentiment in their tributes, many calling Dad the best teammate they ever had. Others stated they had never played alongside a tougher man. At Michigan, Dad might have been an All-American and Heisman Trophy finalist, but self-sacrifice is what lingered as his most respected trait.

The question I have is whether the toughness that earned him the admiration of coaches and teammates was worth it. I want this answer because I saw unrelenting suffering become the cruel counterpart to his earning such compliments.

Whether the result of pride, masculinity, his passion to succeed, or a combination of all three, Dad believed that reaching his football goals required a full-speed charge through any obstacle. If finishing a game meant sprinting back to the huddle for a series of plays that he might not remember, after enduring a collision that his body and brain would never forget, he willed himself to the task. If the chance to play depended on receiving another painkilling injection to mask burning joints, he let the doctor jab the medicine into his body. Knees, toes, or shoulders, Dad didn't discriminate. He welcomed every shot with a smile. The shots brought him closer to returning to the field.[2]

Football's stranglehold on Dad demanded that no alternatives existed. Many years after he retired, he remarked that he still longed for the camaraderie of joining his teammates in the locker room, laughing while having their ankles and wrists taped before a game or practice. Despite the carpenter's set of screws and pins inserted into his body, he craved one more play. It seems that no roadblock could have stopped his life from colliding with football's seductive force. The game gripped him as nothing else in his life ever could.

With success, however, came consequences. By the time he died he had an artificial left knee, an artificial right shoulder, persistent headaches, a mind that had begun to distance itself from reality, vertigo, and carpal tunnel so severe that it stripped all feeling from his hands as he fought to sleep at night. Time and age faded the scars slicing through his arms and legs, but his spoiled joints and pained gait remained. When Dad died, his body was

---

2 Dad loved sharing a story about one particular shot he received in the little toe on his left foot while playing for the Broncos. To paraphrase Dad's words: "The Doc and I got to talking and laughing about this or that while he was busy injecting my toe. I can't feel a damn thing, but he must not have been paying attention because next thing you know, I'm screaming 'Doc, Doc, look.' And he finally looks down and screams, 'Holy shit!' The medicine was dripping onto the floor. The doctor put the damn needle right through my toe."

a junkyard of used parts, a collection of leftovers from a sacrificial offering to his pagan god. Teammates and opponents praised his determination, but our family now lives without someone whose body failed him too soon.

I never felt for a sport, job, or anything, really, even a measure of what Dad felt for football. He worshipped the game and grieved without it every day following his retirement. Perhaps it's unfair for me to question his devotion since it isn't something I can completely understand. Before passing, he told me on countless occasions that he accepted his physical suffering because the toll came with playing the game he loved. I suppose that in his eyes, the desire to reach the pinnacle of his sport meant nothing without a willingness to punish and stretch his body across the goal line to achieve it.

For a long time, I agreed with his perspective. But everything Dad had said about accepting the pain he collected from football changed for me on November 20, 2010. A heart attack too powerful for his body to overcome became his final reward for the toughness admired by fans. On the day he died, his daughter lost her father, his wife became a widow at 55, and I lost my best friend. In the aftermath of his death, I question whether Dad would still choose football if someone had warned him of the consequences. Except I'm sure I know the answer.

"Yes," Dad would say. "All I want is one more play. And maybe one more after that." Then, he would smile.

**Michigan football coach Bo Schembechler and
Dad following the 1976 Michigan season**

CATCH

Growing up in Northwest Ohio with posters of famous football players stuck to the walls of my bedroom and boxes of NFL-player trading cards stacked high in the corners, the fall meant one thing. On Friday nights through junior high school, I would watch the local high school football team and pepper Dad with questions: "Do you think the quarterback made a good throw on that play in the fourth quarter? Did the running back make the right move on that third-down run?"

On Saturdays, I played flag football in the mornings before watching hours of college games on television. Ignited with energy from the games I watched, I tossed a miniature football in the air, jumped over couches to catch it, and dove around chairs in my family's basement. My pretend moves made every imaginary highlight show.

By night, I strained to stay awake to watch the West Coast teams play their games in the setting California sun.

Yes, every Friday and Saturday was great growing up, but Sunday was the day that counted. All week I anticipated Sunday afternoon when Dad played quarterback for both teams in the neighborhood games my friends and I played against each other. I had new pass routes to test and new moves to make. Could I impress my ex-football star pops with my own athletic abilities? I tried to answer that question every Sunday.

Decades have passed since I last played in one of those Sunday afternoon games. Wearing my nostalgia-tinted glasses, the memories appear as perfect snapshots of the cherished youth I enjoyed with a father fully invested in the happenings of my life.

• • •

Church was over. I had survived another service. We'd visited with my grandparents and listened to my Grandpa Lytle tell this week's version of last week's story in a way that made us laugh despite already knowing how it ended. Returning home, I balled up my church clothes, threw them onto my bed, and changed into that day's uniform: black mesh shorts, a weathered undershirt, and an over-sized blue Denver Broncos sweatshirt. I sprinted into the backyard. The screen door slammed behind me. I ignored it. It was game day, and I had scant time for anything but football.

I heard bells ring from the churches surrounding our house. Three, maybe four different sounds, they each signaled the end of Sunday worship and sent their congregations back into the world. Religion might have encircled me, but I considered football fields my real sanctuary and that day's game my real faith. I had waited all week for the Sunday afternoon football game between my friends and me. Dad would play quarterback, and I would shine.

I watched Dad descend the concrete stairs from the back porch while I stood in the corner of our yard. Pale scars decorated the front and sides of his knees. He flashed a smile before dropping his grass-stained boots on the bottom step and sitting next to them. Beaming, he raised both hands in a call for the football that I was spinning in my palm.

His fingers mocked God's vision of perfect creation and defied Darwin's theory of natural selection. His left pinky shot to the side at the second joint, and his index finger bent in an unnatural downward direction. The others curled in swollen, angry ways, each one having been broken during his NFL career.

I tossed the ball across the yard to Dad. He caught it with his right hand. After too many seconds of waiting for him to return the ball to me, I ran across our small yard and stole the pigskin from him.

"About time," he laughed.

"Dad, did I tell you about the highlight catch I had at recess on Friday? It was against the older kids. I caught the ball in the middle of the playground like this." I threw the football to the center of our yard and plucked it from the air with my back facing our brick house. "See, I knew the guys from the other team were chasing me. So I spun like this." I pivoted and dashed five yards before swooping to the right and scoring a touchdown.

"Did you celebrate?" he asked in a tone too serious for my liking. "Remember what I told you about showing off? Act like you've scored a touchdown before. I don't care if it's just recess." I ignored his speech. If I'd heard the old man's call for modesty once, I'd heard it a thousand times.

"Watch this one," I said.

The football soared no more than twenty feet. I caught it and dragged both feet in the grass before they clipped the outline of the concrete patio that occupied a third of our backyard.

"Did you see that? I had one of those at recess last week."

"Reading any books?" Dad asked, ignoring my question.

"Just the ones for school," I said.

"Anything good? I wish I read like you. Don't lose that habit, you know."

"Yeah, I know. You've already told me that."

"Ha. How's school then?"

"Good. Now, watch this play. Michigan's running back did it on TV yesterday. I started practicing it last night."

I tore through the short grass with the football clutched in my left arm. I punched at imaginary defenders with an open right palm. In the middle of the yard, I spun and dove into a pretend end zone. A thin line of green now stained my right leg from knee to mid shin.

"One day, I'll do that for Michigan," I boasted as I returned to my feet. The thought of one day playing for the Wolverines like Dad excited me. I let a wide smile crease my lips. The smile turned out to be short-lived.

"Your mom tells me you never turned in some homework. Is that true?"

"Dad, did you see the Southern Cal game?" I tried to change the subject with a Hail Mary question.

"Homework?" he asked.

"I forgot," I replied and launched the football opposite the steps where my dad now stood. I sensed his eyes shooting torpedoes into my back as I ran to catch the ball. "I thought it was due this week," I lied.

"What's that? I couldn't hear you from so far away. Get your butt over here!"

I turned and took fearful steps toward eyes that narrowed on me. A scowl replaced his grin. If a hole had existed anywhere in our yard, I'd have crawled inside it. I wanted to hide but no escape route existed. Instead, I tucked my chin to my chest and locked my eyes on the ground to avoid Dad's stare.

"Look at me!" Dad barked.

"Yes." I met Dad's eyes. My heart's pace quickened. Even the most elusive football player couldn't escape this trap.

"Look, I know you didn't forget your homework. Remember, all this sports stuff comes second. You're smarter than me. Use football, or whatever sport you play, to give yourself more opportunities. Don't let it use you. School comes first. Got it?"

"Yes," I mumbled, my heartbeat crawling its way back to a normal pace.

"Besides, you know what happens when you mess with the bull? You get the horn." Dad palmed my blond head with his warped fingers and rocked me side-to-side. "Understand?" Dad's smile, now much softer, returned.

"Yes," I said.

"Good. Here come your friends. Let's hit the road before your mom finds something new for me to fix around the house." We laughed together as we walked to our driveway where we met my friends at Dad's rusty Jeep.

"How's the arm feeling today? Better than last week?" they asked.

"Good enough to beat you boys," Dad grinned.

In truth, a botched surgery from his playing days left a vindictive screw inside my dad's right shoulder. The wayward screw used his ball and socket joint as a carving station, grinding the joint and locking his shoulder. Some of Dad's friends used to kid that he could signal for only half a touchdown since that was all the higher he could raise his right arm.

Dad couldn't throw with that arm anymore, but he taught himself to use his left one so he could remain in this game played by a bunch of kids in the sandlot. His self-taught, left-arm throws wobbled from his hand and struggled to reach their targets. We didn't mind. Battered or bruised, we still had a former NFL player as our quarterback.

Inside the Jeep, our Dalmatian, Poppy, waited for us in the front passenger seat where Dad had left her a few minutes earlier before he'd gone inside the house to swap his shoes. I ran my finger on the outside of the plastic windows, playing connect the dots with the smudge marks from Poppy's nose. After opening the door, my three friends climbed into the backseat. I squeezed next to my slobbering seatmate, careful to rent just a small space in an area that she owned. Poppy's nails dug into my pale thigh as she adjusted her position. Her claws scraped my skin, another reminder of my secondary slot in the Jeep's pecking order.

The engine growled for several seconds before we rolled away. After two blocks, we were beyond the reach of Mom's watchful eyes, and Dad pulled into a space along the side of the road.

"Now we're ready to play. Here comes the chewing tobacco!" a voice shouted from behind me. "Game time!"

Dad grinned, mischievous, like a boy who had just swiped a candy bar from a neighborhood nickel and dime store without the shopkeeper catching him. He knew Mom hated his nicotine habit, but she couldn't punish him for doing something that she never witnessed. From the right pocket of his shorts, he grabbed the familiar Levi Garrett pouch. I inhaled the rustic scent and admired the clump of black leaves and twigs he pinched from the bag. Debris flaked to the Jeep's floor as he shook the chunk several times before placing it inside his mouth. In a few chews, I saw a golf ball-sized lump protrude from inside his right cheek. Someday I'll do the same, I thought.

"Remember, nobody says a word about this, especially you." Dad twisted his head and glared at me. "Not a peep to your mom. I don't need to listen to her about this, too," he said, waving the pouch of tobacco in the air.

I glanced around the Jeep. My friends stared me down, firmly in Dad's corner. Even Poppy pressed her paw deeper into my leg. "Don't you dare rat out my old man," she seemed to say. Somehow, I had gained the reputation as a tattletale.

We resumed our drive to the park. I watched as Dad's boots danced between the gas, brake, and clutch. After several hundred yards, he stretched his head out the window and spat a thick, dark liquid stripe of tobacco juice into the rushing wind.

Our drive to the park took fewer than ten minutes. We clipped past three Little League baseball fields and a vacant public swimming pool where weeds had long ago replaced water. Our speed never topped thirty miles per hour, and we saw no stoplights.

We parked in the middle of the half-dozen trees that outlined one edge of the field. Red-yellow leaves littered the ground. Poppy spent a few tongue-flopping, tail-wagging moments with us before sprinting after a pickup truck that coasted through the park's lone road. As with all other weeks, we knew she would rejoin us once she tired from her run. I stood near Dad while my friends raced into the center of the field. The football soon began flying from one buddy to the other.

"Dad, can you smell it? Or hear it?" I asked, bouncing up and down on my toes, my body stimulated by the approaching game.

"What's that?"

"All the hot dogs and burgers on the grills. And the kids playing games, wearing the jerseys of their favorite player. Maybe me." My eyes swelled with excitement as I spoke. "It's the tailgate party for our game."

"Quite the imagination. That's funny because I don't see any kids wearing your jersey," he teased. "Where are the parents?"

"They're off somewhere talking and whining about the coach. Like real life. Everyone's coming to watch us play, like they did for you."

"Is that right? So people will come to watch you play?"

"Yes," I said proudly.

"And what about that homework you never finished? Keep that up and you won't be playing anything. Fair?" Dad's matter-of-factness intimidated me.

"Fair," I replied, the electricity in my eyes subdued but not extinguished.

Banter finished, Dad and I joined the rest of the team. The five of us fanned apart to form a circle inside the approximately fifty-yard field.

"How you guys doing today?" Dad asked my friends.

"Great," they responded, the football passing from one of us to the next without a pattern. "How bad is Ohio State gonna beat Michigan this year?" my friends wanted to know.

"Ha. Don't you wish?"

We pried for Dad's opinion of our favorite college and professional football teams, and he obliged with answers before asking about families, school, and anything else. A black puddle of tobacco juice formed on the grass near his feet as we talked.

We were a mixture of dirt, sweat, grass-stains, and weary legs two hours later after finishing our games. Poppy returned and circled us while we stretched our tired bodies underneath the trees near the Jeep.

My friends and I made plans for the next weekend, everyone agreeing to stay the night at my house. If the weather was nice enough at night, we might walk to the movie theater a few blocks away or maybe play a game of hide-and-seek around the neighborhood. When you're still in elementary school and talking to a girl is a worse punishment than a lifetime of homework assignments, these are life's important topics.

Dad sat near us, listening and not listening at the same time. He looked content, happy to be part of our team. Still, he couldn't be as happy as I was for having a dad willing to play quarterback in the Sunday afternoon football games played by his son and his son's friends. Having Dad present meant everything. Then and now.

A Late-Night Stop

In the late 1980s, Dad and one of his close friends stopped at a gas station in downtown Toledo. The fuel situation wasn't dire yet, but Dad wanted some snacks for the sixty-minute drive home. The hour was late, the neighborhood looked bleak, and the prolific graffiti offered an ominous warning to two men who obviously didn't live nearby.

The friend filled the tank while Dad moseyed inside the convenience store. A thick, metal meshing reinforced the front door, and a small crowd loitered outside the shop. Iron bars protected the store's lone window. Dad's friend tensed as he saw the crowd move inside.

Finished at the pump, the friend waited. And waited. After too many minutes had passed, his concern compelled him to investigate the situation. As he approached the entrance, Dad strolled outside singing a tune of delight. His face radiated as he shouted good night to the cashier and everyone else. Laughs and well-wishers bid him farewell.

"Rob, what just happened?" the friend asked.

"What? That?" Dad chomped at a fresh stick of gum and nodded his head at the store's dissipating crowd.

"Yes, that."

"Well, one of the guys in there noticed my Super Bowl ring and asked if he could see it. So I let him wear it while I shopped. Then he showed it around the store. We all got talking football, and then a few more people came in and they wanted to check out the ring. So they passed it around. It was fun." [3]

"Jesus Christ," Dad's friend said.

---

3 Dad rarely wore the ring he received when the Broncos played in Super Bowl XII because it screamed of posturing. He saved it for specific moments, like when he needed it to start business conversations or, apparently, impress strangers during snack runs.

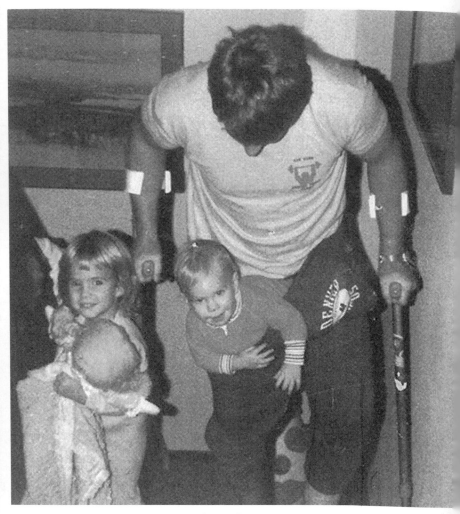

Erin, Dad, and I, circa 1984

Monday Night
Football

I was a regular at Bud's Tavern by the age of nine. Bud's
is a single-story bastion of alcohol and conversation that
sits next to a car wash and Kentucky Fried Chicken on
Fremont's main drag. Dad owned Bud's for a handful of
my younger years in another of his post-football-this-
sounds-interesting forays.

Smoke from too many cigarettes and greasy meals
fried in a makeshift kitchen threatened to suffocate Bud's.
The exhaust system wheezed at best and failed at worst.
The door to the stall for the men's bathroom had been
missing since before I ever stepped foot inside the hal-
lowed walls. Refinement skipped Bud's many years ago,
but character did not. I loved the joint.

My toes tingled and my heart tapped whenever a trip to Bud's approached. Once there, I felt like a prince eyeing his future kingdom while gliding between the bar's wobbly tables. I drank soda from the same eight-ounce glasses as the men used to drink their beer. When my glass ran dry, I strutted behind the bar and sprayed myself a refill from the soda fountain. If I wanted to hang at the bar on a school night and chat football with a bunch of guys looking to let loose, I did that too. Well, sort of, and only on Mondays.

Unlike most elementary school kids, I longed for Monday. Monday meant football games and conversations around subjects out of my league. It meant fatty cheeseburgers oozing puddles of grease onto fries that came along for the slippery ride. Monday, for me, meant Monday Night Football and a trip to the corner stool at Bud's Tavern.

I attended a small, Catholic elementary school through fifth grade. During those years, every Monday morning brought the first mass of the week (the other occurred on Friday). The priest chanted his creeds, and the ritual of service played out according to a well-choreographed script even less enjoyable than the spelling tests I took every Friday afternoon. I watched it unfold with intent eyes that masked my boredom.

Instead of listening, I spent the hour refreshing my brain with the important stats for each team playing in the Monday Night Football game that evening. As the choir rejoiced, my ears heard the old blues numbers that I knew would float from Bud's jukebox. Names such as B. B. King, Muddy Waters, and Eric Clapton didn't mean anything to me at that age, but their guitar riffs helped me escape to a better place than the cramped pew where I found myself on those Monday mornings. My feet twitched against the green padding of the church's kneelers, patience an impossible goal for my energized spirit. A hint of freedom arrived when I dipped my right hand in the holy water collected in a large marble bowl, made the sign of the cross, and left the church thanking God for another night with Dad at the bar. Sports and religion often blurred into one in my family.

When the bell rang at 3:30 p.m. to end another day, I sprinted home and prepared for the evening. I'd finish my homework first and then wait for Dad to stroll through the front door so the night could commence. While waiting, I would imagine my teeth piercing a sizzling cheeseburger, the grease dripping first to my small fingers and then onto my plate of overly peppered fries. The television over my shoulder would show the football game, and I'd slip into the easy comfort of an adult world. That such an image of heaven could exist stoked my faith in God's greatness more than anything the priest had promised during the early morning church service.

Dad and I had a set routine to our Mondays. Two hours before kickoff, we drove to a mostly empty YMCA and re-imagined a basketball court as our football field. Dad envisioned a new "come-from-behind" scenario for our team each week: Down four points with one minute remaining in the game, we had a single timeout and needed to score a touchdown to win. He called the plays and threw the passes. I ran the pass routes and made the catches.

Our offensive charge would start at one baseline of the hardwood court. Without time to huddle, we sprinted to the line of scrimmage between plays. Dad barked numbers that corresponded to specific pass routes for me to run—a secret system developed over several seasons. "One" equaled a "slant," or three steps upfield with a cut to the inside at a sharp angle. "Plant off your outside leg," Dad liked to say. "Two" called for four strides and a break to the sideline, or an "out." "Come back to the football and catch the ball with your hands," Dad reminded me.

Our numbered calls continued into the teens, and I fancied myself a professional player memorizing all the details. I believed that victory depended on perfection with every step of every pass route. Regardless of how long we played, winning and losing always depended on the game's final play. And I *needed* to make the winning catch.

Father and son. Coach and protégé. Rob and Kelly. Our tandem never lost in those days.

I would badger Dad with questions on the short ride from the YMCA to Bud's. "How should I run that route better? Should we add this play? Did you have favorite plays in your games?" I obsessed over every move I made. Dad's confused face now makes me think he probably wondered what type of inquisitive sports-mad monster he had created.

When we entered Bud's through the back entrance, cigarette fumes and familiar voices would collide with my sweaty face. My spirits, already on cloud nine, floated into a world of delight. Belonging inside Bud's, a place that couldn't legally welcome me for over a decade, shifted my confidence into overdrive. Man, this felt good.

"Who's winning tonight?" The welcoming words from scattered patrons buzzed in my ears.

"The team you don't like!" I would joke.

I walked toward an open bar stool. Pictures of Dad and teammates from his glory days covered the walls. In a far corner, a jukebox with rails of flashing lights framing its exterior reflected the neon-blue cursive letters from the "Sweet Home Chicago" sign hanging above it. Smoke exhaled from the tiny grill that masqueraded as the kitchen and existed in a dish room separated from the bar by two swinging doors more fitting for a western saloon than a tavern in Northwest Ohio. Small, four-person tables occupied the floor space. On Mondays, though, the only action worth watching took place at the bar.

As much as I loved football, the conversations at the bar seduced me the minute I settled my butt into my seat. I listened as men spoke in serious tones while sipping beers, their muddled sounds playing like a symphony. Words arriving in rapid spurts, separated by patches of silence, provided the rhythm. Meanwhile, Dad played conductor, nudging the crowd from talk of sports to jobs to wives and the other topics men share when their inhibitions dissipate in the warm glow of slight inebriation. He poked and prodded, pushed questions, welcomed answers. The pace hummed, transitioning from one subject to the next. Dad was a maestro, and I sat spellbound, idolizing the master at work.

As I listened to the swirl of conversations, still naïve about the battles with wives, children, and bosses that leave men with the wounds required to contribute in such situations, I sat silent and happy. Sitting and listening satisfied me. I was more than a wallflower but less than a supporting actor, and that was more than enough.

The two-minute warning of the first half signaled the end of my night. I wished my farewells, and Dad drove me home where my exhausted body collapsed on my bed covers. By the next morning, I started counting the hours until the following Monday. I longed to be part of the team. I couldn't wait to perch atop my bar stool and disappear from elementary school as one of the guys at the bar. Mostly, though, I wanted to spend another evening with my best friend—my dad.

LEAVE YOUR EGO AT THE DOOR

I was sitting in the backseat of Dad's Jeep. Mom and Dad glared at me as two interrogators might pressure a crime suspect. I turned my head, left to Dad then right to Mom, comfort nowhere in sight. My stomach dropped and my heart raced. Dad, the judge, jury, and executioner of this one-sided trial, sat in the driver's seat, his eyes enraged. My ego, fueled by all the hubris a 10-year-old wannabe athletic hotshot can store in his spindly body, had just gotten the best of me following a youth soccer game. Not more than ten minutes earlier, I had boasted to my young teammates and their families of my elite status as the best player on our team. Such arrogance amounted to a cardinal sin in my family, and I would pay the price.

Soccer was never my best sport. The rule forbidding the use of hands during play annoyed me, so I did my best to ignore it. One coach even had me tie my hands behind my back with a shoestring during practices in an attempt to thwart my illegal habit of stopping the ball with my hands before proceeding to boot it. In those days, my wispy blond hair ran afoul of my mom-prescribed bowl cut and swayed above my eyes. To make matters worse, my brain and my feet worked together worse than a rhythmless man stumbling in a soul train dance line. I wanted to kick the ball. It wasn't my intention to trip over my feet and whiff. But it happened. Everything about the sport felt awkward to me.

Thankfully, up to a certain age, soccer games follow a distinct pattern. A player on one team kicks the ball as far as he can down the field. The other players, except the goalies, swarm after it like a mob of mayflies rising off Lake Erie. Since I ran faster than anyone else in the league could, I achieved a small dose of success in a sport where I had no other abilities. I reached the ball first on most occasions and as a result, had the most chances to score.

At that age, though, I thought my fleet-footedness made me the best player on the team. I knew I needed only the right moment to announce myself as the greatest. Have patience, Kelly, I preached during our two months of play. Your day in the sun will arrive.

We played our final game that year in May. After it, the coaches hosted a potluck party in the shelter area of the park whose fields we terrorized all spring. Little stands out about the party until the moment our head coach unveiled the highlight of our celebration: an oversized square chocolate cake covered in white frosting and decorated with bunches of sugar made to resemble soccer balls. The bakery had written the name of every player to the side of a tasty-looking goal and net.

Players and parents gathered around our coach as she gave a short speech to commemorate the season. I watched but didn't listen. My excitement swelled. All year I had waited for the chance to announce my supremacy. If I knew of my greatness, so too should everyone else. Thanks to the local bakery, soon enough everyone would know.

As the coach spoke, I stared at the cake. My name perched on a throne above the heap. It appeared exalted, to me at least, above my teammates. I loved seeing "Kelly" as the first name on the list of players.

The group hushed when the coach finished speaking. Somehow, the opportunity I had waited for all season had arrived covered in frosting in a wilting cardboard box.

"My name's first because I'm the best!" I shouted so everyone, including my parents, could hear. "Look, look!" I pointed to my teammates. "See, they put me at the top because I'm the best on the. . . ."

Life brings with it certain "oh no" moments. I realized in a flash that this would be one of mine.

My declaration finished as fast as it started. From nowhere, a firm hand gripped my wrist. A slight tug arrived first, then a full yank. My body flew away from the party. Disoriented, my feet slipped. I shuffled to regain my balance as Dad dragged me in the direction of our car. I struggled to keep pace. He said nothing, and his silence spoke volumes. I already knew that my words had plopped me knee deep in shit's creek.

Dad's chest heaved with each step. Up and down, in and out, I watched his anger elevate. It seemed that each exhale aimed its fury at me. I thought I'd reached the lowest I could, but then I saw Mom. If Dad wanted to kill me, Mom was outright disappointed. My heart sank, and I began to cry.

Mom climbed into the passenger seat and faced me. Damn my ego, I thought. Damn soccer and damn Mom, Dad, and the baker who put my name on top of the list on the cake.

My heart thumped in sudden bursts against my chest. Tears dripped from the corners of my eyes. Mom observed her fallen son without speaking. I suffered waiting for the car door to open and misery to follow inside with Dad.

Dad entered and sat facing the steering wheel. He paused, growled, and turned. He fixed his eyes on me and waited to speak, his patience a cruel tease. I dropped my head and squared my eyes on my black soccer cleats, my sniffles the only sounds to pierce the silence.

The tension escalated until finally Dad spoke: "I don't care who you think you are. You never say something like that. Don't ever put yourself above any teammate again. Ever! You hear me. This attitude of yours stops now!"

"Yes," I mumbled, refusing to lift my eyes off the floor.

"Now, walk back there and apologize to everyone."

"Come on!" I pleaded without hope. "Can't we just go home? They know I didn't mean it." I lifted my head enough to see Mom shake her head. My whines went nowhere. She refused to take the bait.

"Now," Dad commanded in an eerily calm voice that I'll never forget.

Mom exited the car, pulled the passenger seat toward the front dash, and I crawled out from the backseat. My rubber cleats pressed the blacktop, and I began a slow march in the direction of reconciliation. I kicked pebbles as I moved, hearing laughter boom from the party with every sad, approaching step I took. Carefree and having fun, my teammates were where I longed to be. Parents milled around the table, partially minding conversations and partially supervising their children. I sensed my folks trailing not far behind but dared not twist my head to look.

"Umm," I started when I reached the group. "Umm, excuse me." A small crowd formed around me as a few parents and teammates turned their attention in my direction. "I'm sorry for what I said earlier. I didn't mean it. I'm sorry."

I caught a few glances from uninterested parents and, in a flash, everyone returned to what they were doing before my apology. I had escaped.

"Was that OK?" I asked when I reached Mom and Dad.

"Yes," they said, though their unhappiness remained.

"I'm sorry," I mumbled again.

"We know you are. Just don't ever do anything like that again. Leave your ego at the door next time," Dad said.

"Yes," I agreed.

Mom and Dad visiting me at Princeton, 2004

THE LYTLE MEN

I idolized my dad. No secret there. But Grandpa Lytle, or Popo as his grandchildren called him, was the coolest man I ever knew. Even into his eighties, whenever Popo shuffled into his favorite restaurant, the wait staff would run to his table to shake his hand or give him a hug. Smiles wide, they would laugh—about something, anything. Maybe they didn't even know. It was impossible not to laugh in Popo's company.

On a Saturday morning two months after Dad died, I joined Mom for one of her routine visits with Popo. We arrived at his modest home carrying cups of McDonald's coffee, a stack of breakfast burritos, and a few orders of hash browns. Mom and I sat with Popo talking life and talking Dad. As we ate, Popo rambled through a story that started at the military school in Indiana where he was forced to spend his high school summers, skipped to World War II, flashbacked to his college days in Bowling Green, Ohio, and somehow ended with him causing trouble in bars in downtown Chicago not long before he left to serve in the war.

After an hour, the conversation slowed, and the visit with Popo, sitting in a director's chair across the living room, had seemingly reached its end. However, when I rose to kiss him goodbye, he surprised me. Popo asked if I would stay for a few minutes more without Mom.

Once she left, Popo and I sat for a minute without saying much until he instructed me, "Get me a glass of wine, would ya? And get yourself a beer." Popo was indifferent to the kitchen clock that had not yet reached 11:00 a.m.

"OK." I poured his wine and grabbed myself a beer from his refrigerator.

"Good man," Popo said, his grin—though more subdued than before Dad's death—still lively.

We sat in silence. I knew that Dad had sat with Popo like this during his final years, and I began to realize that Grandpa had asked me to stay to help fill the void. My presence in the house was the closest he could come to recreating the days he had spent with my father. Popo missed his son. I missed my dad. And being together was close enough for us both.

In the 1940s, Popo set the 100-yard dash record at Bowling Green State University. I've read old news articles that said he blazed down the cinder tracks of those days like a lightning bolt strikes the sky. He ran fast enough to sprint neck and neck with future Olympian Harrison Dillard, an eventual sprint champion who won a gold medal in the 100-meter dash at the 1948 London Olympics.[4]

Although Popo managed to best the future Olympic champion in some of their races, he never cared to discuss his track success, preferring instead to recall his antics. "Well, my coach never trusted me," he would say. "He thought I might cause trouble for myself if he wasn't watching. So he made me share a hotel room with him on our road trips. But I remember one time, it was after the All-Ohio meet and the team stopped for food in some roadside town. I had won the 100- and 220-yard dashes, and Coach asked me what I wanted. I told him I didn't want to eat, but that I'd like to go to the bar across the street for two beers. 'Thirty minutes and don't be late,' Coach told me and let me go. Those beers tasted good."

Popo had been one of the world's fastest men in the mid-1940s, but he never boasted. Instead, his stories left you wishing you could have gone out for a night of carousing as his wingman.

Popo lived in Chicago for a short time before his Navy duties took him to the South Pacific. Raised Catholic, he missed neither a last call nor a mass while in the Windy

---

4 Harrison Dillard won four gold medals in total during the 1948 and 1952 Summer Olympics. In 1948, he won the 100-meter dash and ran on the winning 4 x 100-meter relay team. In 1952, he took gold in the 110-meter hurdles and again as a member of the 4 x 100 relay.

City. He told me of nights spent gallivanting around town and mornings attending a 6:00 a.m. service on his way home from the bars. "I snored louder than sin in those pews, but I made mass," he proudly said.

One of my favorite stories of his, though, dated to his high school days and the time he contrived an entire book report, receiving an "A" from his naïve high school English teacher. *Over the Top*, a novel by Guy Impy, became a best-seller in the Lytle house despite both the title and the author being figments of Popo's imagination. What I never told him is that my enjoyment of his lark served as one of my first inspirations to start writing creative stories.

After the war, Popo returned to his hometown of Fremont, Ohio, married his college sweetheart, and raised my dad and Dad's two sisters. For over forty years, he owned the fashionable men's clothing store that bore our family's name. He was the king of all things monogrammed, and since my parents named me after him, I inherited an entire wardrobe of sport coats, dress shirts, sweaters, and satchels that bear our initials.[5]

I think in many ways Popo felt more comfortable with me than he did with my dad. They were close but without the same easy-going bond that I shared with my father. I think that Dad sought too hard for Popo's approval and that Popo had to work harder at being the right father to my dad than he did being a grandfather to me. For many years, a subtle tension lived between them. Over time,

---

5   Popo often referred to us as "Kelly 1" and "Kelly 2."

though, I watched as the ice thawed, and they developed the natural give and take of a father and son who double as close friends.

Popo and I never had this problem. Maybe thanks to our shared name, or because my friends and I spent most of our summer afternoons roughhousing in his backyard swimming pool, Popo and I enjoyed a good-natured rapport. We also bonded through track, the aging sprint champion and his aspiring grandson. From the moment I began competing in Junior Olympic track meets through my last race in high school, I could count on Popo attending. I didn't always win, but he greeted me with his beaming smile after every run.

Popo also had my back as I learned after a brush with the law before my sophomore year at Princeton. I was drunk and foolish on vacation in Ocean City, Maryland, and police officers arrested a friend and me for possessing fake IDs and trying to steal a rusted Bud Light beer sign bolted into the side of a dumpy liquor store. We failed. The cops won. And I expected Dad to drive from Ohio to murder me. Thankfully, Popo knew how to handle his son's fury.

"Rob," he said, as they discussed my arrest, "you're just lucky you were who you were. Think about everything you got away with because you were good at football. Besides, tell Kelly that he has a long way to go to catch his namesake in the trouble department." Then Grandpa flashed Dad the same sly grin that Dad liked to give.

With one sentence, Dad's rage became laughter. With one sentence, I escaped the doghouse.[6]

Later in their lives, Dad and Popo enjoyed a restful weekend routine. On Saturday mornings, Dad would drive to Popo's house and help organize his checkbook, his slate of doctor's appointments for the coming week, and anything else around the house that needed attention. They sat together, Grandpa in his director's chair and Dad on the couch, and watched episodes of M*A*S*H or a John Wayne western. They lived in the comfortable silence of two men so content they needed few words to enjoy each other's company.

Then one Saturday they spent the morning together and ate lunch at a local restaurant before parting. The next time Popo saw his son occurred that evening in the hospital where Dad lay cold on a bed. A horrifying shade of light green had replaced the peach that once colored his skin. Popo sat next to him. Refusing to shed the tears that threatened to overwhelm him, he held Dad's lifeless hand and whispered, "My boy, my boy. Oh my boy."

I sobbed.

Popo sank into his chair, and with my mom sitting next to him, locked his arms with hers. Desperation screamed from every red-eyed face in the room. Soon, Popo began to fidget. He looked at his arm tangled with Mom's and glanced around the room.

"What is it?" Mom asked.

6 Actually, it took one sentence and forty hours of community service.

"Whose *damn* watch is on my wrist?" Popo barked.

"Oh!" Mom shrieked, laughing for the first time since we had learned of Dad's death. "That's my watch, not yours." Then she unwound their arms to show him.

"Oh Lord! Jesus, I thought I was losing my mind!" Popo exclaimed, his sheepish smile a small crevice of light inside a room cloaked in darkness.

I often wonder whether Dad and Popo realized on some level earlier that day that fate intended to cut short their time together. Maybe. Maybe not. Regardless, knowing that Dad enjoyed several of his final hours in the company of his father is something I'll always treasure.

On many occasions, I scoffed at Dad for his weekend visits with Grandpa Lytle, mocking how the two of them sat in such prolonged quiet. It's clear to me now that I was wrong. I had missed all the beauty of those moments. The strength of their bond lived in their silent appreciation for each other. While sitting with Popo on that Saturday morning, two months after Dad had died, I looked past my own pain to see Popo's sadness. I felt how much he missed his son.

As Popo and I sat together in his living room, we watched a since-forgotten television program and savored the other's company—a grandson and his grandfather, one who missed his dad and the other who longed for more time with his son.

Dad's Comeuppance

"The worst licking I ever took playing sports. Let me think about that for a second." Dad wiped his hand across his mouth, considering my question. I was home from college and we were reminiscing over dinner. "It was the time your grandfather kicked the shit out of me in a race when I was in high school."

"What? You raced Popo!"

I knew that Popo had declined an invitation to train for the 1948 United States Olympic Trials after he returned from his years serving in World War II, but I didn't know until that moment that he ever raced my dad.

"Well, I was a senior in high school, and I had just won some big track meet. I was feeling good, getting a little cocky, you know. Football star, scholarship to Michigan, and thinking I was something special. I'd started mouthing off to Dad about this or that, bragging about how great I was. I don't know what set him off, but he got sick of listening to me. So one night after dinner, he told me to put my shoes on and that we were going across the street. I didn't know what was happening, but I played along and threw on my tennis shoes. We headed over to Hayes, and when we got there your grandpa said, 'So you think you're pretty fast, don't you? Won't quit talking about it, that's for damn sure.' I told him that I was fast, and he should check the newspaper. 'That's fine,' he said and told me we were about to race."[7]

"Kelly, I knew your grandpa could run, but I didn't know he could run like *that*! There I was in my sneakers and gym clothes, and he just stood there in loafers and dress pants. I'm heading to Michigan to play football, working out for hours every day, maybe the fastest kid in the state in the 100-yard dash. And there he was, probably hadn't run in a decade or more, and he's telling me to yell go so we can start."

"What happened?"

"Well, I said 'Go' and he blew me away. Our 50-yard race was over before I made it 10 yards. Kelly, your grandpa could run! He kicked my ass."

I never verified the accuracy of this story, but the more I heard it, the more I loved it. Despite suffering

---

7 My grandparents' house, the one Dad grew up in, was across the street from Hayes Elementary School in Fremont. The school's playground included a large grass field where this race happened.

double-digit concussions in football, despite a close loss in the Rose Bowl, and despite a thumping in the Super Bowl, the worst sports licking Dad ever experienced came against a middle-aged former sprinter who had grown tired of his son's attitude.

Well done, Popo.

Dad and Popo carving the Thanksgiving turkey, 2009

Lytleisms

Dad had a way with words. He spoke in obvious contradictions and using proper grammar mattered less than making a point. Dad's sayings, when they worked, delivered their messages in blunt but brilliant simplicity. Here are some of the best.

The polite way to say someone talks too much:
"Their mouth runs like a bird's ass in berry season."

Punctuating a funny story:
"I never laughed so hard in my life." (Countless stories must have tied for first place.)

How to behave:
"Do as I say, not as I do."

Learning:
"You don't know what you don't know. So go know it."

Prowess on the football field:
"Size helps, but speed kills."

Football instructions:
"Hit 'em in the mouth and come out their asshole."

Practice:
"Practice doesn't make perfect. Perfect practice makes perfect. So be perfect."

Improvement:
"Every day you either get better or you get worse. You never stay the same."[8]

Nerves:
"Are you nervous? Good, because if you aren't nervous then you won't do well." (Dad said this about school, sports, jobs, and everything, really.)

Overthinking:
"Kelly, quit overthinking and win the damn race. Everything else will take care of itself."

---

8 Dad borrowed this quote from Bo Schembechler, his head football coach at Michigan.

Playing through pain:

"The only time you're healthy in sports is the first practice of the year. For the rest of season, you're either sore or injured. Get used to it and don't complain."

Expectations:

"Don't expect a medal just for showing up. You have to earn what you get in life."

Perseverance:

"It ain't about what's done; it's about what you do with what's done that counts."

Causing trouble:

"Mess with the bull, and you get the horn."

Hangovers:

"You're of age now, Kelly, so if you want to drink and hang out with the boys, I'm not stopping you. But I want to share something with you that your Grandpa Lytle told me around your age. Your grandpa said that many guys can drink, but Lytle men play it off the next day as if nothing happened the night before. So, if you wanna be a Lytle, don't let a hangover change anything about your next day and you'd better not let anyone see you suffer. I don't care if you spend the entire day making yourself throw up in private or if you cry yourself to sleep at night; make sure the only person who knows how sick you are is you."

Honesty:
"Son, don't bullshit a bullshitter."

Saying goodbye:
"AMF." In Dad speak, AMF meant "Adios, mother fucker."

Dad signed this autograph for Erin
six days before he died, 2010

DID DAD KNOW HE WAS GOING TO DIE?

"Erin, The one I've loved the longest."
Dad
And
"Audie, Love of my life."
Grandpa Rob

Dad wrote these words on two glossy photographs—one to his then 16-month-old granddaughter, Audrey, and one to my sister, Erin. He signed the autographs six days before he died, the last time he ever saw them.

Although Dad participated in occasional paid autograph signings, he generally avoided such outings. He disliked them not because he felt annoyed by any requests, but because he genuinely couldn't grasp how someone could want his signature. "What would anyone do with that?" Dad was apt to say.

He never understood why anyone fussed over him or how someone he never met could be excited to shake his hand, exchange a few polite words, or want his busted scribble on a trading card. In his mind, nothing he had accomplished before, during, or after football warranted such attention. My interpretation was that signing autographs roused the disappointments he felt over a career he never appreciated. Dad never admitted anything this truthful, but knowing the standards he set for his football career—the ones he believed he never met—I don't see this as a stretch.

Family members would ask him to sign something for them on occasion, but unless driven by a special circumstance, charitable request, humorous intent, or as the result of prolonged prodding, he shunned endorsing reflections of his football days for our family. Now that I'm older, it occurs to me that Dad wanted everyone to remember him in the present, not as some glorified football hero augmented by imagination. "You're only as good as your last play," Dad liked to say.

When Dad autographed those pictures for Erin and Audrey without objection, I wondered if my eyes were betraying me. I now question if he somehow knew that death was stalking him.

Dad turned 56 on Friday, November 12, 2010, and my sister and I visited that weekend. Over lunch on Saturday afternoon, we covered the usual fall subject of Michigan and Ohio State football. That evening, Dad worked the sideline first down markers, the "Chain Gang" as he called it, during a high school playoff football game in Fremont's stadium. In hindsight, it was strange that he spent most of the time between lunch and the game sleeping. But in that moment, I paid it little attention. The only thing that struck me as out of place that weekend happened when Dad snatched the black marker from Erin and wrote two short notes.

I remember watching as he considered the football player in the identical action photos she handed him. In the photographs, red spots of blood dotted the padded thighs of his weathered, maize uniform pants. Massive shoulder pads collapsed the navy number 41 of his white University of Michigan jersey. Fissures and chipped paint decorated Dad's Michigan helmet as much as the team's famous yellow wings. Thick, mighty legs charged forward while his eyes flexed through a black facemask to focus on opponents prepared to launch their bodies like heat-seeking missiles in his direction. In the picture, Dad is an aggressive football warrior willing to bleed again for another yard.

After holding the photos in his twisted fingers for a moment, he offered two declarations:

For my sister, he wrote, "The one I've loved the longest."

For my niece, he wrote, "Love of my life."

He reminded Erin that he always will be her adoring father—the one who taught her how to "power color" through first-grade school assignments and the father who laughed and hugged her when she smashed her car into his when she was learning to drive. He was the dad on whose shoulder she cried joyful tears during the father and daughter dance at her wedding. Erin cherished Dad. I doubt she will ever need a reminder of the importance of their bond. If she does, he left her a memorable message with his last goodbye.

For Audrey, whose memories of her grandpa will come from the stories she hears and the pictures she sees, he ensured an enduring memory. One day, Audrey will ask about the framed man in the football uniform. She will inquire about the message of love that betrays the menacing figure.

We will share stories of how her grandpa's eyes sparkled every time she came close, and how he often remarked that she gave him another reason to celebrate each day. When she sees that picture hanging on her wall or resting on her mantle, her mind will ignore the valiant figure in the image, the one whose face hides inside a battle mask, and only thoughts of her adoring grandfather will remain.

I think regularly about these pictures, how the loving words contrast with the fierce running back carrying the football. I wonder if they are a farewell from a man who loved his family more than he cared for anything else. And I wonder if this was Dad saying goodbye.

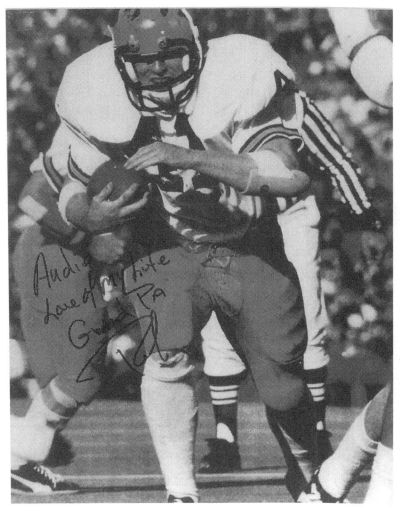

Dad signed this autograph for his granddaughter, Audrey, six days before he died, 2010

FEAR

Not long after Dad died, a friend of his shared with me a collection of anecdotes he had written as a way to remember their friendship. The author, an unorthodox doctor who is as fluent in managing emergency rooms as debating the sixties counterculture movement, sent me his musings in a small, blue moleskin notebook. The scribbled collection revealed pieces of my dad's personality from a fresh perspective. Many stories were unfamiliar while others I recognized as the R-rated version of tales already told to me in PG. I devoured the tangential wanderings of the friend's mind and embraced his vivid imagery.

I read a story, "Fear," one morning, and then immediately reread it.

In his story, Dad's friend admitted that, like almost everyone else I know, he never associated the word *fear* with my dad:

"...there once was a time, and it was just once and brief that I saw fear on his face. This was during what for a better word I'll dub the 'Turner days.'[9] He was based out of Novi, MI, and his office was near my house when I lived there. We made a habit of meeting every week or two for food and drinks. We did this for two or three years.

Part of his work duties took him to Dayton, and one time while driving he had an accident. He hit a guard rail, wasn't badly hurt, but was scared by it in a way that facing a 300-pound lineman, who had an image of him crumpled and moaning in his brain, didn't. We were drinking and dipping into a goo of artichoke and mayo when he confessed he had become scared to drive. . . . his eyes changed, they went into that fear mode. I didn't say anything about it, but the moment impressed me. Rob Lytle was afraid. Oh my."

Following a third reading, I chucked the notebook against the couch on the other side of my living room, my anger stirring. Dad had taught me many lessons. Some he based on compassion and others on perseverance. Some he cooked with a dash of fatherly exaggeration. We never

---

9 During the 1990s and 2000s, Dad worked in sales for the Turner Construction Company and some of their regional subsidiaries.

discussed our fears, though, and I think this was a gap in our relationship.

Maybe I'm wrong. Maybe fathers and sons shouldn't share their fears. Perhaps knowing such intimate points ruins the aura of invincibility that many sons create of their dads. Not that there is anything I can do about it now. Any wish to know more about what my dad feared merely collects dust in the basement of my thoughts alongside other conversations we never explored.

Right or wrong, Dad and I never accepted that we could be afraid. I think we each saw fear as a weakness to avoid rather than a natural, embraceable part of life. In the years since my dad died, I've forced myself to face a number of things (including my fears) that I once refused to acknowledge. They are something I wish I had appreciated much earlier and something I wish Dad and I had shared.

DISCOVERING PORNOGRAPHY

I discovered pornography in May 1996. I was in seventh grade and home alone after track practice while Mom and Dad attended one of Erin's softball games. At 13, and burdened by lusty throes of curiosity, I entered Dad's study determined to search every drawer in every file cabinet for any nefarious nakedness my instincts told me he might be hiding.

An imposing oak desk taunted me as I stood in the doorway to Dad's office. "Boy, don't be snooping where you shouldn't. Your old man won't be pleased seeing his stuff out of place," it called to me. I ignored the desk's warning. I had boobs on the brain.

First, I hunted through the small, two-stack file cabinets on either side of Dad's desk where I found a wasteland of home appraisals and financial statements. Undeterred, I yanked the drawer inside the center of his desk. Nothing, just a silver letter opener and some rubber bands. I slammed the drawer and moved to the stand-alone cabinets underneath the computer table. Empty.

One set of three file cabinets remained. I clutched the brass handle of the bottom cabinet and pulled. It wouldn't budge and neither did the middle drawer. I wondered why Dad had locked them.

Adolescent hope fueled me as I yanked the handle of the top cabinet. To my surprise, it opened, and a world of manila folders greeted me. I peered into and between each folder, finding nothing until I found everything. Sandwiched between the last two folders was a thin book with black binding. On its spine, white letters spelled *Penthouse Forum*.

Jackpot.

I eyed the small book of sin in my hands as a religious man might admire a new Bible. The black lace underwear of the cover model jerked me to attention. Her brown eyes penetrated my young soul. She looked magical, like a goddess created for me to worship. Something inside me jumped. I snapped my head around and listened for footsteps. Silence. The coast was clear.

I braced my body against the hulking file cabinet and flipped to the first story. A small picture of a woman with bare breasts grinned at me from its perch in the page's top right corner. Words like thrust, pleasure, and spasm sparked my imagination. Characters explored each other with their tongues in ways I thought both disgusting and impossible. Their bodies erupted in pleasure, and I *heard* the moans explode from the pages. Although I expected more pictures from my first porno magazine, the lasciviousness of this brave new world captivated me.

Now, I must admit here that I did not go into business with myself right there in the study. I postponed that experiment with self-gratification for another two years. On this day, I read only two stories, thirsting throughout for every plot twist and salivating over every picture. After several stimulating minutes, I placed the magazine back into the cabinet in the exact spot where I had found it. I left Dad's study. My eyes felt dirty, but my body felt good. I wanted more.

For several weeks, whenever home alone, I stole into the study. With every repeat read, I discovered new phrases that fed my titillated fantasies. As long as I returned the magazine to its precise location, I believed my secret remained safe.

Then one afternoon, my favorite magazine disappeared. I checked everywhere in the study but found no trace of anything resembling a porno magazine. Exasperated, I returned to the file cabinet and worked through the series of manila folders a second time. It had to be there. But if it had disappeared, did Dad know about the peeks I'd stolen from his dirty book?

I didn't have to wait long for the answer. On a folded page of yellow legal paper that I missed on my initial search, I found a note scribbled in Dad's handwriting:

"Hi Kelly,

Better luck next time.

Dad."

HAMSTER HEAVEN

Elephants captivated Dad. *Water for Elephants* is the only book I know he read cover to cover. When I asked him why, he said, "I guess I was just rooting for that damn elephant."

I have no idea why Dad revered elephants so much. Once, during my high school years, Dad and I parked ourselves in front of the television on a lazy, snowy Saturday afternoon. Dad operated the remote control and stopped at a show that included elephants. At some point I lost interest and turned to face him, hoping he'd change the channel. He wasn't on the couch. He was staring through the glass doors that led to our backyard, a gentle smile across his face.

"Please tell me you aren't thinking what I think you are," I said.

"What?" Dad responded, sheepishness clear in his voice.

"You want an elephant. Really?"

"I just think it would be fun to have one. As a pet, you know."

"Seriously! What is wrong with you?" I laughed.

"It could live in the backyard."

"You're out of your mind."

"Too expensive you think?" he asked.

I didn't even answer.

"Maybe one day," Dad mused and returned his attention to the television.

Dad loved all animals and though we never owned an elephant, we did own six Dalmatians, three Labradors, one English Setter, one Irish Setter, and more than ten cats by my count. Our house was a flophouse for wayward pets. We rescued stray cats that had wandered to our house and found the free meals so agreeable that they decided to stay.

My parents even became a last resort for our local veterinarian. She phoned us whenever she failed to find a home for one of her dogs. "Sure," Mom and Dad always said. Of course they'd harbor another abandoned pet.

Except sometimes their actions had unexpected consequences.

Sometime during my early college years, my parents rescued a Dalmatian from certain death. He arrived at our house emaciated from years of neglect by his former owners. His ribs pushed against his spotted skin, and he cowered into the first corner available at the mere threat of a hand to his backside. He had learned to survive by scavenging for food, and we realized not long after adopting him that he couldn't be trusted with the other animals in the house, so Mom and Dad kept him isolated from the other animal residents.

My folks' efforts worked until the day they left the screen door to the backyard open, and the Dalmatian bolted after one of our cats frolicking in the yard. Mom recognized the cat's pained snarl and sprinted into the yard to find the dog foaming from his mouth and the cat's bloody tail near his paws. No other sign of the cat existed, so we assumed her for dead. A few days later, Mom found the disfigured feline shivering under a neighbor's porch. The cat needed stitches, antibiotics, and a few days of rest, but she survived and lived the better part of a decade with a wagging stub instead of a tail.

We sent that Dalmatian back to the vet with a note that said thanks, but no thanks.

Animal life as a Lytle wasn't all danger, though. In fact, the common remark from visitors to our house was that no pet had life as easy as a dog in our home. They slept on couches or in any bed they chose. We neither disciplined them nor forced them through any training. If a dog avoided doing anything crazy, such as chomping off a cat's tail, they could expect to live a life in our house beyond any of their wildest imaginations.

Dad doted over our dogs even though they were not his favorite pets. The real head-scratcher is that Dad treasured hamsters. All his life, he treated these furry rodents like royalty. I always found it weird.

As a kid, Dad loved to place whatever hamster he owned in the pocket of his shirt and carry it to the dinner table. He would plop it on the table and watch its tiny legs scurry between plates of food and silverware. More than once, Dad caught a hand to the back of his head from Grandpa Lytle for the ruckus he caused. No matter, though, because the habit continued into adulthood.

Dad owned a revolving door of hamsters throughout our childhood, and George was his favorite. During several Thanksgivings, Dad brought George to the holiday table the same as he had done as a kid. Turkey day at our house included a feast of potatoes, turkey, stuffing, gravy, corn, green beans, and jumbo shrimp dripping with a spicy cocktail sauce. The rat wannabe would poke his tiny head above the crest of Dad's shirt pocket and seem to judge the excess before his pellet-sized black eyes with every whisker twitch.

Not only did Dad cart George around in his shirt, he also insisted that George wish "good night" to our other animals. Dad would cradle George in his hands and press the rodent to the face of the two dogs we owned then. The dogs were agreeable. Mostly they flinched or sniffed at George, blasting him with huffs from their noses in a half-exhale, half-sneeze.

This routine lasted for George's first two years until my family adopted Doc, another abused and abandoned Dalmatian.

Past circumstances had made Doc an aggressive killer. When presented with his first nighttime visit from George, he saw the ball of fur as a delicious treat. With George near his face, Doc popped his jaw open and snapped it closed around George's body.

"Fuck!" Dad screamed as George's hind legs dangled from Doc's death grip.

Dad hammered the top of Doc's head with his fist. Doc, stunned by the blow, released his hold and recoiled. George's rigid body thudded against our kitchen floor. He lay still, lifeless from the attack. Panicked, Dad scooped the tiny body off the floor and dashed into the bathroom, clueless about how to rescue a dying hamster friend. Shock overtook George. Remorse overtook Dad.

Doc's bite had separated George's coat from his body so that it flapped like a fur cape off his back. But somehow, Doc's teeth had not pierced George's skin, and Dad had no outpouring of blood to combat. He rummaged through the medicine cabinet and acted in the most rational way possible for an oft-injured former professional football player: He smothered a cotton ball with antibiotic ointment and applied it to George's bare back, coating as much skin as he could. Dad then pressed George's coat against the oozing medicine and secured the makeshift remedy by wrapping an elastic bandage around the shivering, shocked hamster.

When I asked Dad how he felt when he placed George in his cage that night, he said, "I was sick to my stomach, Kelly. I thought I'd killed my friend."

What a strange man, I thought.

George proved a fighter, though, surprising all of us with his resilience. He could move and stand by morning. Over the next several days, Dad subjected him to frequent "treatments," checking George's coat and applying more ointment as necessary. Eventually, George's fur affixed itself to his body again, and he lived another year after the accident. Other than a faint, jagged scar along his back, the evidence of his near-destruction disappeared.

I suppose after seeing all the effort Dad was willing to expend to keep a hamster going, I was glad he never did get that elephant.

Interesting hair decisions, 1984

THE LOOK

When it came to discipline, the most threatening weapon in Dad's arsenal wasn't his NFL pedigree. It was his eyes. If Erin or I realized we were in trouble, we knew it because of those eyes. Dad never once raised a hand to discipline us because his eyes played peacekeeper in our house.

I never knew Dad to be a violent man. Ornery? Yes. Temperamental? Absolutely, though not about the things one would expect.

As a 16-year-old, freshly minted driver, Erin reversed into Dad's new car, leaving a boulder-sized dent in the passenger-side front door. She expected to spend her last two years of high school locked in her room, but Dad shrugged, indifferent to the damage. "You're OK. That's what matters. It's just a car," he said.

Before my senior year of college, I suffered a more humiliating wreck. Mistaking the gas pedal of my parent's SUV for the brake, I launched it through the front window of a convenience store. I sent the cashier sprinting for safety into the supply room, fearful that the explosive entrance signaled my intentions to rob the place. Two Vietnam veterans who were busy shopping for snacks when I burst onto the scene suffered war flashbacks and someone called an ambulance to treat them. The police arrived and cited me with a failure to control. This was not my proudest moment.

Graciously, Dad let my embarrassment stand as my punishment. "What am I going to do? You're 21 and just drove our car into the Sunoco station store. You're a smart kid, so you don't need me to tell you how much of an asshole you look like. Your friends will punish you enough."

But when the moment for discipline did arrive, Dad's eyes reigned supreme. "The look," as Mom named it, occurred at the terrifying moment when Dad narrowed his glare onto a single subject the way a noose tightens around a neck. His lips would purse and his nostrils would flare like a rabid animal high on a cocktail of venom and crazy. The eyes became blue-green bullets of menace.

I remember my first experience with "the look." I was in eighth grade and Dad had been out of town for a few days on a business trip. Before he left, he had asked me to finish some chore that in an act of early teenage disobedience, I ignored.

"When I ask you to do something, I expect it to get done," Dad told me when he returned. No harm done to me, just a brief tongue-lashing from an irritated father. Except I let my teenaged "how dare you confront me" attitude triumph over my better judgment.

I can still picture myself standing in the doorway to my bedroom, a scowl planted on my face. Dad turned his back to me, and as he walked toward the stairs, I thrust my right fist into the air with my middle finger pointed to the sky. My actions screamed, "You can't tell me what to do." I enjoyed my act of defiance. Then Dad suddenly snapped his head around, and I nearly wet my pants.

"Oh no! I'm sorry! I'm sorry! I'm sorry!" I squealed, backpedaling into my bedroom.

"'Oh no' is right," Dad said as he charged at me with the ferocity he once reserved for the football field.

Our bodies choose between fight or flight in times of panic, and in this instance mine chose flight. By the time Dad reached me, I had scrambled into a small space below the yellow wooden desk that occupied the back corner of my bedroom. All that separated me from death was the wobbly chair I clutched with my hands as a barricade.

"Get up!" Dad commanded.

"No," I whimpered.

"Get your butt out of there."

"No," I whispered.

"Now!"

I pushed the chair back and crawled out from under my desk. When I stood, I forced my eyes to connect with Dad's the best I could. He glowered at me for what seemed like eternity. His eyes disappeared into crazyland. "The look" eviscerated me. My knees rumbled. My hands trembled. A chill crawled up my back. Knots curled in my stomach as I waited for fury to arrive from the feral-eyed monster I had provoked. My heart threatened to thump through my rib cage. This is how life ends, I thought.

Then Dad's scowl slipped and the cocked smirk more familiar to his face returned.

"Don't ever do that again," he said.

"Yes."

"Ever. You read me?"

"Yes."

The moment passed with that exchange. Dad let an amused chuckle escape his mouth as he left my shriveled spirit to collapse onto the blue comforter atop my bed. Residual terror from a beating that never occurred stripped my body of all its might. I survived, but I feared that "the look" and I would spar again one day. It took four years.

On the Friday following Thanksgiving of my senior year, I attended a high school party with several friends at the home of a classmate whose parents were away for the weekend. A vanilla-scented fog of Black & Mild cigar smoke filled several rooms in the house. Empty cans of Natural Light and Bud Light filled the trash cans and kitchen counter.

I was the designated driver, and after a few hours I left the party to drive a friend to his house. My friend, also sober, had a basketball scrimmage the next day and needed to be home in time for curfew. When I returned, two police cars with flashing lights had infiltrated the fun. I owed another buddy a ride home, and since I had not been drinking, I sauntered inside the house without any fear of trouble from the cops.

I recognized the officers standing in the kitchen, and I immediately noticed that a rapid cleanup job had removed the beer cans from any visible locations. The icy chill of teenage tension had replaced the earlier revelry. The cops avoided arresting anyone but ensured that the party ended. They asked if I could drive a few people home, which I agreed to do.

Following this police-mandated jaunt around Fremont, a friend and I reached home 30 minutes past my 12:30 a.m. curfew. We rummaged through the refrigerator hunting for an easy-bake pizza or nacho-making supplies. Nothing tempted our taste buds, so we decided a late-night drive to Taco Bell would quell our hunger pains. I grabbed the car keys from the counter, but before we could leave heavy feet pounded down the back stairs that led to our kitchen.

"You're not going anywhere," Dad snarled before he came into sight.

The second he turned the corner into the kitchen and faced me, four years of suppressed fear roared to life. "The look" had returned. Before I could speak, my friend darted into another room—the brute force now staring me into submission had panicked the poor kid.

"We were just going to drive to. . . ," I started.

"I don't care where you think you were going. I want to know why you're late."

"Well, the cops busted the party, and they . . . ." My attempts to explain the unique predicament failed.

"The cops?" Dad questioned.

"Yeah, well, the cops came to the party, and since I wasn't drinking, they asked . . . ."

"Were you drinking? Why can't you answer me? You're story isn't checking out."

"Just let me talk," I pleaded.

"Fine. Talk."

"When the cops broke up the party they asked me to drive some people home. That's why I'm late."

"That's wrong. You're wrong. The cops would never do that. Quit lying."

"I'm not," I begged. "I had to drive . . . ."

"I don't want to hear it. You're lying. You aren't making any sense. We'll deal with this later." Dad stomped upstairs to bed, leaving my corpse in the kitchen.

I trudged into the family room and found my friend tucked into the corner of the couch.

"I ran in here the minute I saw him look at you. Dude, what was that?" He appeared still shaken by the encounter.

"I know," I said. "I know."

Sleep escaped me that night. Every time I closed my eyes, I saw Dad's menacing look demanding answers. Saturday arrived without punishment as we avoided each other, only heightening the anxiety. Apparently Dad had decided to let me suffer a slow death.

I tucked myself into a blanket of dread and tried to sleep on Saturday night. Sunday morning, when our family had taken our customary seats in a pew near the rear of our church, I spotted one of the cops whom I had helped a few nights earlier sitting two rows behind us. I wondered if his presence meant good news or bad news. Eventually, I decided that things couldn't get any worse.

When church ended and we stood to leave, the young officer stopped my dad. "Hey Rob, I wanted to say thank you for Kelly's help the other night," he said. "I'm not sure if he told you, but he bailed us out."

"Yes, he told me," Dad begrudgingly replied, his face a mix of frustration and amusement.

"Well, just thought I'd say thanks," the officer concluded.

Hallelujah. My messiah had arrived in the form of an off-duty police officer. A large grin creased my lips. I looked at Dad and shook my head in mocking satisfaction.

"Ha! I told you!" I boasted as we exited the church.

"Shut up and quit smiling," Dad said, shaking his head. "Look, I'm sorry for not believing you," he continued. "You got me this round. I'm sorry."

Dad had the character to admit his mistake. As for me, I won a showdown with "the look," and victory felt good.

LIFE ON THE SIDELINES

Life on the sidelines is a lonely place for a sports-crazed kid struggling to cope after losing a high school football season to a knee injury. Just 17 years old and three months removed from reconstructive surgery to repair torn ligaments and cartilage inside my right knee, I was standing between cars in a parking lot in Toledo, Ohio, when I collapsed and sobbed away a youth's worth of frustration. I felt lost and alone, desperate. In that moment, Dad clutched my fragile shoulders and changed everything with two simple words.

It would be a gross understatement to say that sports played an important role in my life. Dad was everybody's All-American, a high school football star turned collegiate icon. He finished third in the voting for the Heisman Trophy after his senior season at the University of Michigan and graduated as the school's career leader in rushing yards. He was the first man to score a touchdown in the Rose Bowl and the Super Bowl. After his retirement from the NFL, our family left Denver and returned to my parents' hometown of Fremont, Ohio, where I grew up in the shadow of his accomplishments.

Accepting the importance of athletics in my life was more formality than real decision. As Dad's only son, I bore the pressure that came with wearing his last name on my jerseys. When I demonstrated an aptitude playing sports, they became part of my inherited identity. The first time I ever made the Fremont newspaper, a picture showed me running with a football at a local high school camp. The title read, "Like father, like son." Coaches and adults around Fremont called me "Little Lytle," out of reverence for Dad's achievements. Playing sports became an addiction, and I was a preadolescent junkie.[10]

An old saying around my house went like this: "Practice doesn't make perfect, but perfect practice does." I trained for perfection in football, basketball, and track.

---

10 I see my childhood differently as an adult than I did as a kid. Growing up in Fremont under the weight of Dad's accomplishments caused me to internalize a suffocating pressure to succeed athletically. I took the standards that I felt others set for me and raised them. The need for success burdened me in ways only hindsight allows me to see. I wanted to be so good at sports that people stopped thinking of me as Rob Lytle's son and started thinking of him as Kelly Lytle's dad. I competed subconsciously against this thought every day while I practiced football and basketball or trained for track. Satisfaction was impossible to attain because I was chasing an unbeatable ghost.

During my elementary school summers, I spent an hour each morning practicing basketball ball-handling drills, marking the time with two episodes of *The Wonder Years*. I threaded a basketball around my head in circles and passed it in figure-eight patterns between my legs. Kevin and Winnie had their first kiss and first fight in the background of my drills. Once finished, I moved outside and launched ten jump shots from ten different cracks in our driveway at the basket attached to our garage. I separated the sets with ten free throws and tracked every made or missed shot. If I missed too many, I penalized myself by running sprints around my neighborhood block. My best free throw percentage came in just south of 90% during those morning shooting sessions—pretty good for a fourth grader.

In the afternoon heat, Mom and I drove to the high school track where I prepared for the weekend track meets I competed in every June and July. I laced up my tiny, orange Adidas sprinter spikes, doused my short blond hair with cold water, and exhausted my legs during grueling workouts on a blacktop surface harder than most roads. Dad scripted each workout, listing everything from the times I should run to the length of breaks I should take between each sprint. He adapted my training from routines he completed while a college sprinter for Michigan. Mom timed everything, and we reported the results back to "Coach" each night. I kicked benches, rattled fences, and launched water bottles across the track when I ran slower times than the workout suggested, but I never considered quitting. Somehow, too, I even craved more, so I competed on traveling baseball and basketball teams. The rugged workouts and regimented schedule seem sadistic now, like a tariff on being youthful and energetic, but aside from the handful of verbal outbursts I unleashed during track workouts, I embraced everything about it.[11]

A need to exceed the expectations set by my last name burned inside me. Competition mixed with my passion to excel. Combined, they seduced my compulsive nature. The athletic successes I earned stimulated my ego and hooked me on sports. My life buzzed so fast between training and competing that I never considered any different path.

By my sophomore year of high school, I started receiving recruiting letters from colleges for football, basketball, and track. Major schools with marquee names that competed in the best conferences contacted me. Would I play football and run track in the Big Ten? What about Stanford, Notre Dame, or Virginia? Maybe one of these schools would become my college home. The plan I had set in motion in elementary school to receive multiple college scholarship offers in multiple sports was within my grasp. I would have my choice of both where I wanted to attend college and what sport I would play.

---

11 I made the decision to train relentlessly on my own. Although Dad never explicitly forced me to obsess over how I did, his history, excitement over my successes, and the bond we forged through sports intensified my obsession.

But everything changed in the summer before my junior year when a crossover dribble in the final seconds of a high school basketball tournament separated the alphabet soup of ligaments inside my right knee. Doctors offered a dreadful prognosis for any athlete: a torn anterior cruciate ligament (ACL), a partial tear of the medial collateral ligament (MCL), and bucket-handle tears of the medial and lateral menisci.

The surgery to repair my knee lasted over four hours. I woke from the anesthesia delirious and spewed vomit onto my hospital gown. I dropped into sleep again somewhere mid-puke. A few hours later, after the fog from the knockout medicine lifted, I writhed in pain around the hospital bed. My leg burned like 500 pounds of enraged firewood ready to burst into flames. I had to pee but the muscles I needed to use to go to the bathroom had entered hibernation following surgery. Drugged, sad, and needing to relieve myself, I asked my parents the most important question of my life up to that point: "Will I ever play sports again?"

"Of course you will," Mom and Dad assured me in unison, even going so far as to share stories of other athletes who overcame worse injuries. As they spoke, I saw tears collect in Dad's eyes. Jesus, I remember thinking. This is the first time I've ever seen him cry. A sick feeling unlike anything I had ever known blindsided me. Even in my haze, I knew my parents had just lied. They were clueless just like me. In that moment, I believed my sports life had received its death sentence.

And I still couldn't pee.

Over the next three months, anger, frustration, self-pity, and fear assaulted me in turns. I knew no outlet for these emotions so I bottled them away in places where only I could find them. Wherever I went, I told people how well I was recovering and how I expected to return to the varsity basketball team that winter. Everything I said was a lie, though, because I shivered at the threat of altering my sports-obsessed life.

Sports had been my closest friend since I had started playing flag football in second grade. Without sports, I felt deserted, as if that friend had abandoned me without a warning or a promise to return. On the outside, I remained the same smiling kid I had always been. On the inside, I felt like a capsizing ship trapped in stormy waters. I had no compass, no life raft, and nobody to guide me home. I needed help, but I didn't know how to express my fears—not even to Dad, someone who had experienced the anguish of sports rehab throughout his career.

As my anxieties became more distilled, I realized that I still believed I would compete again in sports, but what I really feared was coming back and no longer excelling. How could I be part of a team but no longer a star? This question stalked me at every turn.

While I internalized my fears, two other emotions came to full boil. The first, a searing jealousy toward my teammates, fed the second, which was loneliness. Any happiness I felt for my friends still playing that football season came with limits. Their successes challenged my competitiveness. Although I hoped my teammates performed well, I wanted them to come close and lose. If they lost, it was clear I remained an important part of the team. If they won, I was replaceable and forgotten.

During the first months following surgery, I realized that athletics—and life—march on regardless of the participants. On the sidelines and removed from the game's outcome, I loved hearing people tell me I was the missing link between the team winning and losing. Their words were a shot of helium to my deflated ego. My small-mindedness during this stretch of recovery disturbs me to this day.

Handling my loneliness was trickier. At 17, I thought a man's toughness must be without cracks so I hid my isolation and allowed no one inside—not Mom, not Dad, and not my friends. I didn't know what to say to them. How could I let anyone glimpse my eroding rot? Everywhere I went I felt alone.

Three months after my knee reconstruction, my emotional cauldron boiled over. Seven games into what should have been my junior football season, the team prepared for one of its most challenging tests of the year on the home turf of a respected rival and their all-state running back. Our locker room hummed with nervous energy before kickoff. I wandered by myself through a sea of friends having their ankles taped. I watched their heads bob to music playing from inside their headphones. Fists pounded shoulder pads and hands slapped to wish good luck. Eventually, a quiet focus enveloped the team inside the locker room. Determined stares foreshadowed the fine game they were prepared to play. It was our purple and white against their blue and gold. I wore a uniform of khaki pants, an unused game jersey, and white sneakers on the sidelines.

We took an early 6–0 lead and held it until late in the fourth quarter. Keeping their star running back and speedy wide receivers from reaching the end zone took an entire team effort. I watched with veiled jealousy as my friends ran, blocked, tackled, and covered the opposition with more zeal during that game than they had shown all season. After the clock reset to zero, resentment conquered my happiness. I felt excited they had won the biggest game of the year, but I hated being an outsider to their success. On the field, with sweat and dirt clinging to their jerseys, players embraced in exhausted exultation. I stood in quiet detachment away from the team, half-listening as the head coach praised the victory. Tears stung inside my eyes, and I drove them deep into my stomach's pit.

Inside our raucous locker room, I drifted through cheers and animated embraces. The stink of damp socks and trampled grass reminded me that I played no role in the victory. A pasted smile on my face remained until I left the locker room red-eyed and combustible, my presence as unnecessary there as it was on the field earlier. I hobbled on a swollen knee to the parking lot where Dad stood waiting to drive me home.

We walked in the direction of his car in silence, moving through crowds of other parents busy congratulating themselves on the team's win. At the car, I stopped and let three months of tears unleash in a storm down my cheeks. I demanded answers. Why did I have to miss the season? Would I ever play sports again? What use was I now without the games I loved?

In that moment, Dad did the best he could. He wrapped me in his arms and said nothing for several minutes while I wept. He let me exhale the sadness I'd wanted to show since the operation. Then he spoke the two words I needed to hear.

"I know," he said. "I know."

Dad knew because he understood my suffering firsthand. For six of his seven NFL seasons, he had buried his pride and watched his teammates play the game he cherished without him. Other players practiced together, won and lost together, and celebrated together, but injuries kept Dad on the sidelines. He endured operations, physical therapy, and years of rehabilitation to rejoin the team. For some reason, his efforts always failed. Dad's loneliness and frustration became part of his personality, sharing space alongside his humility and sense of humor.

Now he watched as his son experienced the same emotions that still tormented him fifteen years after leaving professional football. Yes, I was only in high school, but desperation can exist at any age. Since the injury, Dad had suffered alongside me, internalizing my pain as his own. Now, with two words, he lifted me off the sidelines and put me back in the game.

We made the sixty-minute drive home in silence, having already said everything to each other that we needed to say. By 8:00 a.m. the next morning, Dad and I walked into the weight room together and continued the unceasing task of rehabbing for future sports seasons. After the previous night's catharsis, I relinquished the defeat of my past and faced the challenges placed before me, this time with my teammate by my side.

Like father, like son

Kelly Lytle, 6, the son of former Ross High School, University of Michigan and Denver Broncos running back Rob Lytle, runs past several defenders during a six-on-six game at the 10th St. Joseph Central Catholic Crimson Streak Football Camp at Sacred Heart Wednesday. The camp is the largest ever, with 88 participating. Six high school coaches are providing instruction with help from 10 SJCC players. The camp began Monday and runs through Friday.

News-Messenger/Eric Brands

Football camp, 1991

Walk Before You Run

I spent six weeks on crutches from mid-July through August letting my knee heal following the surgery I had before my junior year of high school. "Use the crutches until you feel comfortable walking," my orthopedic surgeon had told me as he gauged the stability of my leg before determining whether I could begin walking. The doc said it might take two or three days until I gained enough confidence to walk without them. Since school started in less than a week, I figured if I could move without crutches by then it would be progress. As I soon learned, Dad had a much different schedule in mind. He made sure I knew it, too.

Less than five hours after the doctor gave me the green light to ditch my crutches on the condition I felt comfortable enough to walk, Dad and I ventured to my

school's weight room for separate rehabilitation workouts. In April of that year, Dad had had his right shoulder replaced.[12] While I completed my knee exercises, he
stretched his shoulder to regain the range of motion it lost
when a botched operation first froze it in the mid-1980s. I
lost count of the hours we spent together during that summer and fall, our beaten bodies both grimacing to return
to some less bruised shade of normal.

"I thought the doctor told you to start walking," Dad
said as I stepped off a five-foot tall collection of rusted
metal pieces welded into a menacing-looking exercise
apparatus that appeared as if it belonged in a bad horror
movie but was actually designed to work out one's triceps.
The wooden crutches that I needed to move crisscrossed
each other on the floor no more than three feet from me.
I hopped on one leg to them.

"He did. See."

Facing Dad, I slipped the crutches under my armpits.
I pressed the rubber base of the poles into the floor to
support my body weight and moved in measured steps. I
didn't trust my repaired leg, and the crutches had become
my security blanket during the six weeks I had spent with
them. I had never recovered from any surgery, let alone
the infamous ACL reconstruction, before this operation.

---

12 I remember the exact date of Dad's shoulder replacement because it
occurred on April 20, 1999, the same day as the Columbine High School
massacre in Colorado.

The thought of facing repeat destruction when I started walking panicked me.

What happens if I collapse or my knee erupts a second time? Would that mean another round of anesthesia and pain in the hospital? Would I suffer more days pinned to the couch in a dark living room with a cold cloth draped over my forehead, nauseated from the migraine that accompanied my pain medication? If I step and my knee fails, would more seasons of my high school sports career dissolve before they started?

"What are those for?" Dad asked in a serious tone. He stepped a handful of paces to where I leaned on my crutches, nodding at my support beams.

"Huh?" I played dumb.

"Those things," he pointed straight at me and not the crutches.

"I haven't walked in six weeks. I need them."

"Got it." Dad scrutinized me as he spoke. I saw neither anger nor frustration in his face. He looked resolved, committed to finalizing some still forming plan.

"What?" I asked with as much force as I could muster.

"Give me those," he flicked his head at the crutches.

I relinquished my grip on the sticks, handed them over, and watched in horror as Dad heaved the crutches. They crashed about fifteen yards away against an archaic exercise machine unused except as a coat repository in the corner of the room.

"What was that?" I shouted.

"Go get them!"

"What?"

"You heard me."

"What are you talking about? You're crazy. I can't walk over there."

"Go get them. And if you limp once, you start over. I'm watching every step."

Dad always had a crazy streak, but now he'd turned maniacal. Who was he to think that after not walking for six weeks I could meet his cold-hearted request? What a prick, I thought, and tried to incinerate him with fireballs from my eyes. He merely smirked, then chuckled, indifferent to my ire. God, he could be a glorious bastard.

The scar tissue that had accumulated inside my repaired right knee meant I could bend it only partially. My leg couldn't straighten, either. Still, it supported me when I pushed off my right toes. This first solo step infused me with confidence. I continued toward the crutches, quickening the pace with each body lurch. My healthy leg led the charge, dragging its damaged partner behind it. I might have wobbled like Tiny Tim minus the cane and hat, but I was on the move.

"Stop!" Dad barked after allowing a few yards of my hobbling.

"Why?" I snapped.

"Because you're walking like shit, that's why. Now get back here and start over. I don't care how long it takes, you have to walk perfect."

"Perfectly." You know you aren't in a power position when correcting grammar is the lone weapon in the arsenal.

"Cut the attitude," Dad said.

"Asshole," I mumbled loud enough for Dad to hear.

"Slow down and go get the crutches the right way. Now!" Dad's cocked grin infuriated me.

"Yes," I relented and walked with slow, proper steps for the first time in six weeks.

This time, I chopped my normal stride into tiny fragments. I imitated an actual walk as much as the stiffness in my right leg would allow. Anger at Dad and at the injury fueled me.

I considered summoning all the force I could from my sweat-soaked, 150-pound body and taking a swing at my father. He deserved a whooping. Somebody needed to put the despotic dictator commanding my walk into place. Except I did nothing. I realized it didn't matter what I did. Dad would have just laughed at me.

I spent my long walk of misery cursing him in whispers instead.

We stood in silence for a minute after I reached the crutches. Dad broke the ice.

"Look, I've been there," he said. "Too many times. Rehab sucks. It's miserable. It's lonely. But you have to do things the right way every day. Like walking without any hitch in your step. You can't limp or baby it. You have to learn to walk without thinking, like before. Make it natural. If you want to play sports again, like you said you did, then trust me. Do the work the right way or else you'll end up favoring your leg and just injure yourself again."

"I got it," I said.

Although my teenage brain wanted to argue about everything, I understood that I should agree. Dad knew sports, and he knew about recovering from injuries to return to sports. A method existed somewhere behind his madness, even if the way he delivered it riled me. While ailing in my hospital bed the day after the reconstructive surgery, I had vowed that I would endure any work necessary to recover and play as I did before the injury. If I wanted the chance to compete in college athletics, days like this one were necessary.

Dad could infuriate me with his teaching style, but I knew that everything he did for me, he did with my best interests in mind. This experiment was no different. As I've grown older, I find myself often returning to this moment. When times get difficult or when goals seem too daunting, I know that two choices exist: fold my cards and retreat or put in the effort required to improve.

PROFOUND ADVICE

I remember being a high school senior and sitting on the couch one Saturday watching college football games as Dad approached the room shaking his head. His face wore a frustrated sneer. "This is miserable," he said, rolling the sleeves of his striped, button-down shirt halfway up his forearms. "Last thing I want to do tonight is go to whatever it is your mom has planned." He huffed before snapping his head around to make sure that Mom had not heard him.

"Mom pick your shirt out too?" I asked.

"Yeah. Of course she did, ass." After twenty-three years of marriage, he knew the battles to concede. "What are you doing tonight?"

"Just staying here."

"Really?"

"Yup."

A hint of disappointment flickered in Dad's eyes. I was 18, had plenty of friends, and was utterly boring. No parties beckoned. No girls cared. Youthful, reckless fun existed somewhere, but it didn't include me.

Dad considered his next words for a few seconds. Confusion, and maybe some suspicion, crept across his face.

"Where are your friends?" he asked.

"Not sure. I think they're with some out-of-town girls they met a couple of weeks back."

"Oh really. Why didn't you go with them?"

"I don't know. Didn't want to."

"Why not?"

Dad's curiosity annoyed me. The truth was that I preferred solitude because girls intimidated me. Independence offered a better option than a night spent stressing my brain for interesting things to say, only to have it refuse to cooperate and instead spoon-feed my shaky voice humdrum questions about school or other boring subjects. Girls sped my heart's beat into a sprint and turned my head into a landfill of second guesses. I used aloofness toward girls as protection from the horror of having to speak to one.

"Those girls are annoying and slutty. I didn't want to waste my time." I said as convincingly as I could.

Dad placed his left hand over his mouth and rubbed his face. His eyes dropped and he exhaled several deep breaths as he considered his next move. When nothing came to mind, he turned and left the room the way he had arrived.

After a short walk toward the hallway, he pivoted and faced me. Rebelliousness touched by a hint of coolness swept over him. Dad had some guidance, maybe, or perhaps a sprinkle of wisdom to pass from father to son. Whatever it was, his body language suggested that the thought pleased him.

"You know, sometimes it's just nice to get laid. Keep that in mind."

Dad chuckled as he left the room.

Smart-ass, I thought then. Smart man, I understand now.

Please Make It Stop

I slumped in the passenger seat of my family's car. My head throbbed. The skin below my red, weary eyes was puffed. My chapped lips opened to a voice gone raspy from the claws of dehydration scratching at my throat. No matter how many times I brushed my teeth (and I had already done so three times), my mouth stank of cheap beer, and my tongue tasted of cheaper whiskey. It was 8:30 on a February Saturday morning. I was 17, suffering a massive hangover, and facing a rehab workout with my ass-kicking father as my partner. The stone-cold look locked on his face said miserable exhaustion awaited me.

In my house, if you made a commitment—especially to something sports-related—you stuck to it no matter what. I had bargained with Dad to let me stay at a friend's house the previous night. He agreed, but made me promise we would be working out by 9:00 a.m. I don't recall specifics, but I imagine it finished with him saying, "That's fine if you want to stay the night. But if you want to get your knee healed, you'll get your butt home in time to work in the morning."

So there I sat, my head against the window, praying for God to intervene somehow. The sins from the night before bubbled in my stomach, a volcano waiting to erupt in a confession of teenage offenses. I'd spent most of Friday evening slugging beers and gritting my teeth after downing harsh shots of whiskey, vodka, and any other liquor my friends and I could procure. My insidious decisions had delighted me at the time. Now I faced an endless string of exercises with a father who achieved athletic success by outworking his competition from high school through the NFL.

I was ruined. I knew it, my body knew it, and as I learned soon enough, Dad knew it. I felt vomit crawling up my throat.

For the next three hours, Dad assailed me with an assortment of muscle-taxing movements. The torture started with a twenty-minute warm-up session on a stationary bike: five minutes of easy pedaling, ten minutes of intervals (where I alternated pedaling against high resistance for one minute and recovering on a lighter setting for the next sixty seconds), and a five-minute cooldown of easy riding.

Sweat glistened across my forehead. Jack Daniels threw a tantrum inside my head. Faintness swept over me as I stepped off the bicycle. The bike ride had cleared the cobwebs from the previous night's alcohol, but pain and nausea were now my closest friends. I needed something to unleash me from Dad's grip. Maybe a quick death.

The real workout commenced with single leg squats. Three sets of twenty-five repetitions on each leg, with a fourth set of twenty-five for my injured right leg to over-work it in an attempt to rebuild the strength it lost when reconstructed. Lunges next. I stretched forward, then back, then forward, then back, in a monotonous loop that ran without end. "Mercy!" my muscles called, but no one heard.

Fires raged from my thighs to my hips to my head. My right leg quivered with each exaggerated lurch. When Dad said stop, I stood upright and stretched my legs, which wobbled like the wheels of a broken grocery cart. When I moved, I stumbled into a squat rack the way a drunk might stagger against a bar's walls on his way to the restroom.

I bent over, placed my hands on shaky knees, and gasped for every spare bit of oxygen in the musty weight room.

"That's the ticket. Good work!" I heard Dad shout. Leave me alone, I thought. Just leave me alone.

As I found a rhythm and moved faster through the workout, Dad directed me without sympathy. Leg presses to leg curls, leg extensions to wall sits, calf raises to a collection of exercises designed to stress my hip flexors. Sweat coated in cheap beer soaked through my shirt. My hands shook as I fumbled to adjust the pins that controlled the amount of weight on each workout machine. Dad watched in silent amusement while I labored from station to station.

"Be perfect," he said. "Never sacrifice form." A veteran of knee rehabilitations, Dad knew if I was working as hard as I needed to or loafing. "Stop," he shouted if I cut any corners. "You're cheating. Start over and do it right."

"I can't," I pleaded. "My leg's shot."

"Fine. Rest and use less weight. But then you start over. And no cheating this time. You won't fool me." Dad smiled with graveness in his eyes as he spoke. He raised his eyebrows and nodded his head. I knew not to cross him.

For several seconds, I sat on a bench and regrouped. With my head turned down, I realized that my fatigued, bloodshot eyes had admitted to Dad every underage alcoholic drink I had guzzled fewer than twelve hours earlier. He *had* to grasp the extent of my hangover. Worse, I think he relished the fact that I knew that he knew about my transgressions.

When we reached the halfway point of that day's rehab, I chose not to celebrate. I had no room for wasted energy, not with the most difficult exercises still on the horizon. Instead, I stole a short breath and dragged my body toward the water fountain. My arms dangled, lifeless, at my side. My fingers twitched uncontrollably. Two withering Jell-O molds had replaced my legs. As cramps seared into both calves, I doubted if I could even make the short walk necessary to reach the fountain. When I arrived, I stuck my face into the stream and let the water rush over my forehead and onto my flushed, defeated cheeks. The cold offered a reprieve from the suffering suffocating me. I made a mental note that any fun the prior night was not worth today's pain.

Phase two of the workout started with my least favorite drill—dot (or star) jumps. Five dots on the floor formed a 3 x 3-foot "X." An exercise guru had invented a variety of patterns one should jump through on the X to increase speed and quickness. I despised this unknown man.

Using muscles that desperately wanted to collapse, I moved in zigzags, figure eights, circles, and X patterns. I jumped and twisted off both legs, bouncing around the tiny space on a single leg like some handicapped kangaroo hopping half-drunk to nowhere. Intervals set at thirty seconds of action and thirty seconds of rest eviscerated my will to fight. When I closed my eyes during the breaks, I saw bright white stars twinkling against the blackness.

"Faster. Move faster!" I heard the old tyrant a few feet in front of me cry, his eyes engrossed in the sin-stained kid before him. Dad wore a leather jump rope around his neck and operated a stopwatch in his right hand.

"Time," he said when the routine ended.

"Thank God!" I screamed and dropped to the rubber floor.

"Get up. You're not done yet!" Dad shouted and helped me stand. A thin, slippery puddle of perspiration and remorse outlined my body's form at my feet. My shirt smelled like a mixture of junior high gym class and Sunday morning frat house.

Dad tossed me the jump rope and the intervals began once more. Jump for one minute on the right leg, then rest for thirty seconds. Jump for one minute on the left leg, then rest for thirty seconds. Repeat three times. "Run" in place with the jump rope for one minute, then rest for thirty seconds. Repeat three times. Complete two turns of the rope in one jump for one minute, then rest for thirty seconds. Repeat three times. Finally, jump for one minute at top speed before resting for thirty seconds. Repeat three times.

At last, I stood below the entrance to the weight room and exploded through a routine of single leg jumps that would conclude my pain. "Smack the wall! Jump! Explode!" Dad yelled. "Don't favor your leg! Keep jumping and hit the wall!" Dad bellowed as I collected my last ounces of effort and propelled my body into the air for multiple sets of ten jumps on each leg, careful to smack the wall above the doorway or else Dad would discard the jump.

When I finished, I dropped to one knee and stared at the floor. I clutched my shirt over my face and screamed in silent, agonized triumph. My limbs felt like a melted stick of butter, but at least I had finished the workout. After a few minutes, I locked the weight room doors and headed to meet Dad, already outside in his car.

"Nice job today," he said and tousled my soaked head with his hand. "Really good, actually."

Seriously, I thought. Had I been wrong about Dad figuring me for a hungover idiot? Maybe my secret was safe. Had Dad somehow not noticed that I had spent the previous night overindulging on booze with friends?

When we reached home, I grabbed a Gatorade from the refrigerator and plopped onto the couch. An exhausted, satisfied feeling washed over me. Dad kicked my butt in the workout, but I had escaped without punishment for my partying. Pride in my accomplishment filled me.

Then the hammer dropped.

"Good job today," Dad repeated as he entered the living room. "Next time, and I mean this, don't show up fucking hung over!" Great mother of God. He knew all along.

"What?" I looked his way, feigning as much confusion as possible.

Dad locked eyes with me for several seconds until mine retreated. "You heard me. Next time, don't be hung over." He left the room and never spoke again of the moment.

Only a junior in high school at the time, I missed the full significance of Dad's message. I thought then that I had skirted any real punishment for breaking the law. Dad had unleashed his fury on me in a merciless three-hour workout. But who cares? I never puked, I never quit, and I weathered the worst of it.

Now I see that Dad struck a firmer punishment than I first realized, and that it aligned with the goal I had set after my orthopedic surgeon had repaired my knee. I wanted to return to sports and play well enough to compete in college athletics. I had school records to pursue on the track, and I planned to star on the football field and basketball court for my high school.

The lasting meaning I take from this insufferable, hangover-riddled morning is that temptations of short-term pleasures threaten everyone. They tease and taunt until they victimize us. To envision a purpose worth achieving means avoiding these negatives. It means staying focused on the long-term effort necessary to conquer the hurdles in our path.

That Saturday morning, without an iota of lecturing, Dad provided me with an unforgettable lesson in the sacrifice required to achieve a goal.

**Dad with Bob Hope at an All-American
banquet before Dad's senior season, 1976**

AIN'T TIME TO QUIT

I started playing organized sports in second grade. From that time on, practicing football, basketball, or track became my passion. I set strict schedules for myself and followed arduous routines, each day dictated by a thirst for improvement. When I reached high school, success came as the natural extension of the sacrifices I had made to prepare for the athletic career I craved. I earned seven varsity letters in track, football, and basketball. I qualified for the state track meet three times, placing fourth as a freshman in the 4 x 100-meter relay and seventh in both the 100- and 200-meter dashes as a junior. My time of 10.5 seconds in the 100 meters set a school record.

Playing football, I averaged nearly ten yards per carry as a running back, and schools such as Notre Dame, Virginia,

Stanford, Princeton, Purdue, and many others inquired about me playing for them following graduation. My athletic achievements, combined with my 4.0 GPA, allowed me to be selected Academic All-Ohio three times. Interestingly, I accomplished much of this *after* tearing my ACL, MCL (partially), and medial and lateral menisci in my right knee, among the worst injuries an athlete can suffer.

The devastating twist, though, is that I accomplished all of it *before* I tore the ACL, MCL (partially), and medial and lateral menisci in my other knee while avoiding a defender on a simple sweep play during the third game of my senior football season. In the two previous games combined, I'd scored five touchdowns and rushed for over 400 yards. My fantastic start to the season was over. Injury demolished me again.

On Friday, September 8, 2000, several hours after my left knee erupted, I stretched across the couch in my parents' living room with two ice packs wrapped around my knee. Mom kissed my forehead before she went to bed. I sobbed the moment she left the room. I knew that the dream I had nurtured since second grade of playing sports at an elite level in college was probably toast. How many high school kids recover from two knee reconstructions in less than two years and compete in Division I college football or track? Worse, I knew my prize for putting the junior year knee injury in my rearview mirror was a months-long victory lap full of quivering leg muscles and hours rehabilitating alone in my high school weight room. A misery I'd already experienced awaited me.[13]

Later that night my mind careened between anger and despair. Why me? Why again? What now? I searched for hope in my hopelessness as my brain leapt to the effort, isolation, setbacks, small victories, and large defeats waiting for me. I recalled the days I languished in a dark room after my first surgery, vomiting from my pain meds while begging for anything to extinguish the fire torching my leg. I revisited all the nights I spent watching the clock click to the small numbered hours of the morning, torturing myself with worries over an uncertain athletic future. I knew that on the spectrum of problems facing people in the world, mine rated firmly in the "who gives a shit" category. Still, to a 17-year-old kid who had spent his entire life playing sports, knowing so early in life that one of your dreams is shot is dispiriting. When I finally fell asleep, I knew that rehabbing this injury would be a battle physically and a war mentally.

Devastation filled me when I woke the next morning, but I refused to sulk. Instead, I coined a half-rhyming, grammatically butchered catchphrase: "Fuck it. Ain't time

---

13 I eventually realized my goal of competing in college athletics by running track for Princeton University. My sprinting career never lifted off, though, and after a third knee surgery and myriad other setbacks, I stopped running after two seasons. I claimed that I quit from the collective toll of too many injuries. But I really quit because my ego couldn't handle the sting of being only an average runner. My foolish pride may be a topic for another book.

to quit," I told myself before setting the goal of not only competing in Ohio's state track meet that June, but also winning either the 100-meter or the 200-meter dash.

Two days later and less than thirty minutes after MRI results confirmed the initial diagnosis of my wasted knee, I drove to my high school's weight room where I sweat through sixty minutes on a stationary bike. I forced my leg to make full cycles through the swollen stiffness that fought it at every turn. Gunshots of pain burst from my injured knee. I pedaled harder. My surgery remained more than two weeks away, but I had no time to waste if I wanted to reach my goal.

I started walking without crutches in November, six weeks after surgery. Sometime in January, I shuffled down a basketball court at the local YMCA, learning again how to run. Every day I encountered the same routine of one hour of rehabilitation before school, a half hour at lunch, and three more hours after school. I grimaced through my exercises, shouted at weights too heavy for my weakened leg to move, screamed at everyone and no one all at once, and concealed inner tears.

During track season that spring, my times slowed, my knees ached, and my conditioning suffered. When I trained, I could taste the anesthesia from surgery rising in my throat and threatening to spill onto the track. I could sprint barely 200 meters without feeling my lungs scream for air and my legs wobble. Competitors that I once beat now easily ran past me, and I heard whispers from runners on other teams wondering why I was no longer as good as I was the season before.

Frustration ate at me. It seemed that no matter how hard I worked, I would never achieve my goal. Still, I started every morning by saying the same thing: "Fuck it. Ain't time to quit."

Finally, in early June, the pop of a starter's pistol sent my legs flying around a red track for the finals of the Ohio high school state 200-meter dash. I didn't win. Not even close. The first place finisher dusted me halfway through the race, and I had no prayer of catching him. I did manage second place, though, and after two knee reconstructions in less than two years, the silver medal was something I was proud to achieve.

At the conclusion of the race, Dad was standing with my sister behind a short fence to the right of the finish line. I turned and saw him as I collected my breath. His jaw was open and his eyes were wide. His smile beamed proudly. My second-place finish had shocked him. Dad, of all people, understood the effort it had taken to reach that finish line and how much the accomplishment mattered to me.

Our exchange lasted for only a second, but that moment sits atop a special pedestal. I will celebrate it forever.

WARM MEMORIES OF A FROSTY NIGHT

Dad could be ornery and obnoxious, stubborn and opinionated, but he was a good man with a kind heart. And I remember one blustery January night when I had a first-class seat to witness his compassion.

I was approaching 10 years old, and on this evening Dad and I had attended a basketball game at Fremont Ross, the public high school in our small town and Dad's alma mater. As the game was ending, the two of us exited through the wooden double doors of the school's gymnasium. We walked down a small hallway surrounded by trophy cases. I counted three pictures of Dad from his high school football days. My head lifted and my smile broadened. It was awesome to be in the presence of a sports legend.

Outside, a black, icy night and a howling wind smacked our faces. I pulled my stocking cap over my ears and jammed my bare hands into the front pockets of my yellow and blue University of Michigan jacket. Our shoes skidded across the slushy parking lot as we made our way around the visiting team's bus to Dad's mustard-colored Jeep. The rusted collection of iron and metal looked tired, but I knew the four-wheel machine could chug through the slick streets that threatened our drive home. After I climbed inside, I cranked the heat to full blast and rubbed my small hands in front of the vent, which blew only cold air before it rumbled to life. I watched, shivering, as smoke from my breath evaporated in front of my face. A voice from the local radio station called the end of the game. The Jeep's plastic windows, secured by metal zippers, vibrated in the wind. They overwhelmed the chattering of my teeth.

Less than a mile from home, Dad jerked the Jeep into a U-turn and slammed it into park under the glow of a "Used Tires for Sale" sign.

"Why'd we stop?" I whined. "Just drive home."

"Hold on a minute," Dad said.

I watched him stare at a stalled car about thirty feet ahead from where we had parked. A youngish man stood bundled in a heavy coat next to his dead car, and I could just make out the outline of a woman in the passenger seat. A dim streetlight broke the monotony of the evening's darkness.

Dad opened his door and a gust of snow blew inside before he could slam it closed. He moved toward the helpless couple, his rubber boots cutting large imprints into the snow. His shoulders shrugged as he reached the man. A brief conversation ensued, and soon I found myself crawling into the backseat to make room for two outsiders in our now crowded Jeep.

The arrival of strangers to our car didn't frighten me; it drove me mad. I figured Dad could handle any danger thrown his way by the newcomers, but I was cold and tired. I wanted to get home. Dad's little act of charity wasn't helping matters.

The mood in the Jeep grew relaxed, cheerful even, as the newbies laughed at some joke from Dad. Their conversation focused on the basketball game and the winter storm as we slid through several snowy streets before reaching a gas station maybe a mile from where we had found our new friends.

Dad walked inside the convenience store to purchase a small, red plastic gas container. He filled it while the two strangers and I waited inside the Jeep for him to finish. I scrunched my body deep inside my jacket in the backseat and wished my father's heart were as cold as my toes. We could be home already, I thought, and I could have my body submerged in a hot bath, the sizzling water tickling my frozen skin alive. Instead, I was shivering in the backseat of an icy automobile, forced into the role of quivering bystander and watching Dad assist people I knew we would never see again. Get me home, I begged in silence.

Dad wore a wide, toothy grin as he filled the small container. I couldn't tell if he felt genuine happiness over his actions or simply enjoyed toying with my winter-induced callousness. Regardless, how he could have so much fun at this moment was lost on me.

When we returned to the couple's car, they offered a heartfelt thank you and tried several times to pay for the gas and aid. Dad refused their money, saying it was his pleasure to help and that he enjoyed meeting them.

We watched as the man filled his car's tank and then made tracks down the empty, snow-covered road. When we returned home, I took my bath and thawed my bones. Soon, the colors of the evening's escapade blurred into the background of my dreams, and Dad and I never spoke of the evening again.

Despite my frustrations during the experience, I now cherish the lesson I learned during that frosty night more than twenty years ago. Dad rescued two strangers without a promise of notice or reward. His simple gesture of kindness, made without hesitation and even with some glee, showed the true meaning of compassion. I was fortunate enough to witness it.

Accomplice

Football obliterated dad's body. He admitted to me that he had suffered double-digit concussions, and I know that doctors repaired his damaged tendons, ligaments, and joints in almost thirty surgeries. Traumatized nerves shot incessant throbs of pain inside his head. His arms and fingers tingled somewhere between asleep and numb. His nights were battles between a brain that needed to rest and a body that said no. Dad couldn't sleep, but it pained him to stay awake.

Dad suffered from a functional addiction to painkillers for at least the last thirty years of his life. Whenever I watched him ingest another pill, I told myself that he needed the medicine to survive the turmoil stirring inside his body, a turmoil he endured without regret because of his love of playing football.

Besides a fondness for chewing tobacco and an over-indulgence in Swiss cheese, Dad had few vices that I witnessed. He indulged in a few beers on occasion, but unless he was having dinner with friends, enjoying the holidays, or visiting me in college, I never saw him drink alcohol. He loved his pills, though, and craved the escape they offered. After all the years he committed to football, I convinced myself that without the endless trail of prescription meds he wouldn't survive his day-to-day routine.

I have no medical degrees, but I have to imagine that a reliance on Vicodin, Lorcet, and Oxycodone contributed to Dad's premature death. I believe that after all the years the narcotics spent churning through his bloodstream, they wreaked enough havoc to contribute to the massive heart attack that caused his death. Dad surrendered his body to football in a career that spanned two decades from youth leagues to the professional ranks. For almost three decades after his retirement from the game, he sucked down tiny white devils to withstand the lightning strikes coursing through his veins.

Mom fought to cure Dad of his addiction. Better than anyone else, she understood the lurking consequences. She flushed fresh prescriptions down the toilet only to see refills arrive the next day. She cried and yelled, "Rob, you have to stop! Please, for me, Rob, go see someone about this." Day after day, year after year, Mom pleaded with Dad. Every day she battled him. But she did it alone.

"Oh Mom, leave Dad alone," I said more times than I care to remember. I mocked her tears. Mom had the strength to fight for, and against, her husband. I ignored the issue and offered excuses. Now, I'm saddled with my regrets.

Unfortunately, my actions got worse.

I admired my dad's threshold for pain. In this, I suppose I'm not much different from any football fan glorifying his favorite player. Dad's aches stood out to me like merit badges in an athletic career full of accomplishments, and I used his debilitated body in the endless game of paternal superiority that sons play. I presented Dad as more than a former NFL player. He was a survivor, a fighter who proved his mettle every time he swallowed another pill and grimaced through another day. His resolve, I championed, had no limits. Rather than demand he seek help, I approached his dependence as a building block in the "my dad is tougher than your dad" ascent to manhood I hoped to make. I wore his addiction as a personal accomplishment and ignored the toxins his heart pumped upstream against each day.

I can still remember weekends spent watching football with friends during and after college. "Want to know about football?" I would ask rhetorically, craving attention from my peers. "Then you should see my dad's hands. All broken and disfigured. Same with his knees. He's a functional painkiller addict, too. That's how tough he was to play the game." I used Dad's suffering as a trump card to own the room and elevate my self-worth. I have too many of these memories. Looking back, being young, selfish, and irresponsible is my defense.

One part of me wants to find a scapegoat for the abuses Dad sustained, to focus my anger in that direction and clear my conscience. I want to blame the culture of football, which celebrates its game-day warriors as if they descend from Greek gods or are the living heirs to the Colosseum of bloodshed once inhabited by Roman gladiators. Football heroes fight through their pain. If not, they place their manhood and legacies at risk. The great ones are heroic despite their injuries. Sitting on the bench means another player throws their passes or makes their tackles. Someone younger and healthier waits to take their position in the firing squad once the first cracks appear in their shields. For my dad, standing on the sidelines as an oft-injured bystander tortured a man too reliant on football successes for his happiness. He faked smiles and laughs to hide despair's dogged destruction of his psyche.

Like lambs to the slaughter, players step between the white lines and devastate their bodies. But I can't blame Dad's painkiller addiction on the sport he worshipped. Dad chose to play football. He knew its risks, accepted its consequences, and until the day he died wanted one more play from the game he loved.

A passion for playing football drove much of Dad's life. He needed to play, and he needed the competition. If playing meant he would suffer grisly consequences later in life, then he welcomed those costs. Football's physical, bonding nature captivated Dad. Scars, screws, pins, and painkillers were the calamities he accepted for his sacrifices. I should have said something about his usage, a sentence here or a plea to stop there, except I was too self-centered to accept the task. In my warped mind, I appreciated Dad's pain because it made me feel better.

I used my dad's addiction as a stamp for my own superiority. The words I spoke to boost my standing illuminate all the discomforting pictures I see inside my head, the ones where Dad reaches into the pocket-sized black nylon bag where he carried a rosary and his pain drugs. In these images, Dad grabs another small white pill. He places it in his mouth and swallows. I stand in the background, accepting his addiction with my inaction. Later, when the moment better serves me, I will applaud his dependence with my boasts to anyone willing to listen.

There are nights, helpless ones, where I sit alone wondering what Dad thinks. Can he ever forgive me?

WE LEAVE FOOTBALL; FOOTBALL NEVER LEAVES US

Dad stared into the NFL Films' camera, his eyes serious. He smiled, paused, and said, "We leave football; football never leaves us."

It mesmerized me to see my father's turn in the ensemble of former players interviewed for this particular NFL highlight film released sometime in the mid-1980s. The scene crystallized his place in professional football in a way that watching his game films and the handful of highlight videos we owned never could. Dad looked more human in this clip, more like the man I knew than the football player of his past. I was probably 12 the last time I watched that video. What I never could have grasped at that young age is how much this quote summarized Dad's post-football life. More, I had no idea how much it influenced mine.

Two decades of playing football at its highest levels burdened my dad with a physical imprint impossible to miss. What most people never saw, however, was the mark that exiting the game had left on him psychologically. Dad reached the summit of his profession only to suffer through six injury-riddled seasons of the seven he played for the Denver Broncos. When he removed his cleats for the final time, he left the game bitter over how his career had ended. Neither time nor other accomplishments could quell this profound disappointment.

Few people can pinpoint their life's dream while still a child. Fewer still experience the triumph of attaining their specific goal (this number shrinks even more when the goal is to play professional sports). The odds are too long and the road too onerous. As my dad always said, making the NFL took a little skill and a lot of luck.

Still, Dad had a singular mission to play football. Reaching the NFL was the attainable target that made all his sacrificial sweat worthwhile. When football stopped, when his days in the sun had vanished, he saw his dream collapse in a heap of missed opportunities. When Dad retired before the age of 30, he did so on terms dictated by someone else, the game having inflicted upon him a lifetime of wondering "what if" and "what could have been." Football quit my dad, but he never quit football.

The cheers faded, the limelight burned out, and the questions over what to do next remained. Football had defined Dad for most of his life. It offered a steady routine of practices, games, rehabilitations, and trips to the operating table. On Sunday nights, after another frustrating game earlier that day, he languished in a Denver townhouse with the lights dimmed, his mind replaying opportunities lost. He begged to God and my mom for a different outcome. Mom, to her credit, propped him up as best she could, as she did throughout their relationship. But football owned Dad and dictated his mood. If the game went south, he traveled to the same depths. This frustration, despite its misery, somehow gave oxygen to his life. He craved everything—all the brutality and all the suffering, all the joy and even the heartbreak—that football provided him. Even at its most painful, football gave Dad his identity and his purpose.

When Dad retired, the football player who once set the standard for playing through pain at one of college football's greatest programs needed his wife to wrap her arms around him as he sobbed through sleepless nights. In the daylight hours, he played the role of retired professional hero. He adhered to an outdated code of toughness that he believed everyone expected from him and hid the anguish shredding every finely tuned muscle fiber in his body. In private, he cried tears that spoke the most honest words possible of how leaving football had left him in emotional ruin. Football had been his great love, and besides our family, it served as the glue that held him together. After the game had tapped all his useful force, anguish blanketed him in thoughts of what once was and what would never be again.

Mom did everything any person could do, and then more, to help Dad. During the first years after my family moved to Ohio from Denver following Dad's retirement, Mom and Dad would listen to *Memory* by Barbara Streisand on an antique record player. While Dad wailed in the dark over the love he lost, Mom carried him into the light of each next day. Mom's strength kept Dad afloat. Her resolve kept him fighting against his hopelessness. Dad needed Mom's bravery when his fled.

In the years to follow, Dad meandered through a series of unfulfilling jobs, thirsting for something that could inspire in him a satisfaction approaching the one he found playing football. He managed a clothing store, ran a bar, worked in banking, and sold professional sports arenas and stadiums for a national construction company. Although he achieved some measure of outward success, none of his roles ever mattered to him. He spent his post-football life running from career to career. With each change came Mom's unflinching support. Even into the week he died, twenty-six years after his retirement from the NFL, Mom helped Dad search for something that could fill even a sliver of the hole he felt in his life without the purpose football brought him.

Many times, I wanted to ask Dad if he realized how his decades of soul-searching might have trivialized almost forty years of Mom's life. Although he never had this intention, I believe his frustrations relegated a portion of his time with Mom as unfulfilled. She stood by him during years of abundance and years of famine, but somehow he always needed *more*. I wonder if Dad ever considered the selfishness of his frustrations. I wonder if he ever realized how much Mom suffered alongside him.

My sister and I faced a different situation. Erin and I were fortunate children. Dad doted on us unlike any father I knew. We never questioned his love or appreciation for us, and we each grew to idolize him for different reasons. Despite my gratefulness, it frustrates me that he never found enough satisfaction, even in my sister and me, to accept his life as complete.

Selfishly, I see Dad's pursuit to replace football as an inescapable burden in my life. I'm obsessed with fulfillment and meaning. Nothing I've done—graduating from Princeton, working on Wall Street and in the NFL, writing, or volunteering in children's hospitals—has ever satisfied me. The weight of Dad's post-football "passion quest" hangs over me. I wonder if I'm chasing after purpose for both of us.

Replacing football was impossible for Dad. I get that. But his inability to relinquish the game after retiring has left me questioning why the lives of my mom, my sister, and me failed to provide enough. Dad would scoff at this thought, but what I feel doesn't change.

A phrase I hear often is that the NFL stands for "Not For Long" because the average career for players is only three seasons. My experience living with a father who lasted seven years in professional football suggests a flaw in this comment. Retiring from football left Dad with permanent wounds because his "Not For Long" turned out to be forever.

**Mom and Dad celebrating his Wiseman Trophy
as college football's best player, 1976**

LOVE

The 1982 NFL season, Dad's sixth in the league, began on September 12. Mom woke that morning, nudged Dad, and signaled with her eyes that today would be the day their son arrived.

"Please, Tracy, you've got to be kidding me. Not today," Dad said. His Denver Broncos kicked off against the San Diego Chargers at 2:00 p.m.

"Oh yes, today. Soon. We need to go," Mom replied. They raced to the hospital together and by 1:17 p.m., I entered the world.

The Broncos then arranged a police escort for Dad from the hospital to Denver's Mile High Stadium. Dad sprinted through the tunnel and reached the sidelines in time for the opening kickoff. The team welcomed me into the Bronco family over the public address system, and cheers erupted from an oval-shaped sea of more than 70,000 fans in orange and blue. Dad blocked a punt during the game while Mom watched from her hospital room holding her healthy son. Life for my family was good.

Bliss, though, is often short-lived. Nine days after I was born, the NFL Players Association went on strike, and a few weeks later Dad transformed my mother into an obscenity-spewing, frying-pan-swinging, frenzied version of her traditionally calm self.

With the strike inhibiting the players' ability to train, Dad and one of his teammates decided they would spend the morning exercising at a local sports club to stay in shape for whenever games resumed. Dad left Mom at home to care for my 2-year-old sister and me.

Hours passed. The morning slipped to afternoon before fading to dusk. The phone never rang. Mom was sure that Dad wasn't in real danger, at least not the type that comes from trouble with the law, so she assumed he and his dear friend were crisscrossing Denver's saloons drinking cold beer. After midnight, fifteen hours since Dad had left the house for his workout, Mom heard someone fumbling with keys at the front door.

Mom found Dad's drunk, sorry body plastered to the front porch, where he had tumbled while trying to open the door. An overhead spotlight illuminated his splayed picture of athletic imperfection.

"Tracy! Tracy!" Dad belted.

"Where the hell were you?" Mom attacked.

"Tracy! I fell!"

Mom retaliated by dumping a bowl of cold peas on his head, an act that provoked more of his laughter.

With Dad swimming in a shallow pool of peas, Mom snapped at his friend, a 6'8" tight end. When the friend retreated from the porch to the front yard, Mom dashed after him, swinging a frying pan as she cursed him to the afterlife and back again. In the Denver night, two figures carved figure-eight patterns through the small, suburban yard. One, a hulking football player, pleaded for forgiveness from the other, my typically forgiving mother, who berated him with a potpourri of savage swears.

Dad spent that night and several others on the couch. Eventually, Mom forgave him and the story became one of those epic tales that somehow arrived in conversation during every birthday or holiday celebration.

Mom and Dad had their spats. They fought over bills and money. Dad ignored Mom's questions about his day, and Mom annoyed Dad by inventing new ways to ask them. They tested one another, but they also loved each other deeply.

Mom supported Dad as he coped with retiring from the kid's game he cherished. She balanced his outward bravado by being the gentle, considerate ear he needed when his guard dropped. Mom challenged Dad to be more compassionate, encouraged the shaky confidence he struggled to maintain, and helped show him how to become a better, more sensitive husband and father.

Dad gave Mom the strength she needed to be herself. He nurtured her sympathetic nature while encouraging her strength of conviction. If a day turned difficult for Mom, Dad consoled and pushed her through her challenges. He listened, and that is a lesson in itself.

My parents weren't perfect, but they were close to being perfect for each other. I was fortunate to see true love every day in their relationship. I know what love means because of them.

● ● ●

Love is a couple meeting in high school when a shy girl asks the star of the track team if she can borrow his starting block because the girls' team doesn't have one. Love is the smitten boy saying yes.

Love is an All-American high school football recruit avoiding the calls of coaches from Ohio State, Michigan, and Notre Dame because he is busy digging tunnels through the snow with his girlfriend and would rather spend time with her than listen to promises of his future football greatness.

Love is the high school girl who ignores teachers when they tell her to dump her boyfriend because they believe that boy is an arrogant troublemaker.

Love is in the letters the star freshman football recruit sends his girlfriend after leaving home for fall football practice. Love is in the inner fragility the strong man shares only with her.

Love is the woman who trusts her heart enough to forget the words of strangers who tell her during the first week of college classes that her relationship with a Michigan football player will fail during the first semester.

Love is a girlfriend who stays awake late the nights before her boyfriend's football games, eating double-fudge ice cream with her best friend because they are both too nervous to sleep.

Love is pronouncing "I do" to your high school and college sweetheart. Love is committing to a life together until death makes you part.

Love is a wife attempting to make Boston cream pie from scratch because she knows it's her husband's favorite dessert. Love is the husband who says thank you and eats the scrambled mess of cake, custard, and chocolate glaze as if it were prepared in a professional bakery.

Love is a husband hitching a ride on the back of his friend's snowmobile through impassable Denver roads during a Christmas Eve blizzard while clutching the toy refrigerator his wife wants to give their daughter the next morning. Love is the husband saying he would do it again in a heartbeat.

Love is standing in your wife's delivery room before the birth of your first child wearing a sweat suit and carrying a clipboard and stopwatch to time each contraction.

Love is staying at your wife's side as she gives birth to your second child on opening day of the NFL season. Love is ignoring the police escort waiting to rush you to the game until you're positive that your wife and son are healthy.

Love is sitting in the waiting room while a doctor opens your husband's knee or shoulder for another operation. Love is accepting that this surgery means months of painstaking rehabilitation and more tears over whether your husband should even bother trying to play professional football anymore.

Love is a wife who sits in Denver's Mile High Stadium to watch her husband grasp at the dying remnants of the dream he has chased since before you met. Love is hiding in the top row to avoid the stinging criticisms fans unleash at your husband on the field.

Love is supporting your wife in doctors' offices around the country as you embark together on a mission to understand what her lupus means for the future of your family. Love is always saying yes when she wants to try a new treatment or doctor because your sole care in the world is her health.

Love is absorbing your husband's tears and offering him support as he falters in the aftermath of retiring from professional football. Love is prodding him to heal despite knowing that nothing will ever fill the hole in his heart now that he has lost his other great passion.

Love is a husband subjecting his hair to a perm and his arrhythmic legs to dance lessons because he wants to show his wife he cares.

Love is flushing down the toilet your husband's prescription pain medication because of their terrifying long-term effects. Love is forcing your husband to take vitamins, blood pressure medicine, aspirin, and joint-healing pills in an effort to thwart the trauma assaulting his body.

Love is supporting your husband through a series of job changes and his questions over his worth and purpose. Love is never letting him forget how much he matters to you and his children.

Love is a husband and wife washing dishes, their hands reaching for dirty plates together in the same bubbly sink, after another family party on Christmas Eve.

Love is a husband who laughs and jokes with his mother-in-law so everyone can remember her smile even though Alzheimer's has stripped her memory. Love is the husband who drives his father-in-law to see heart and lung specialists and keeps the man's spirits high despite deteriorating health and an uncertain future.

Love is a wife interlocking arms with her father-in-law in the hospital as he pleads with God to answer why it was his son's turn to die and not his own. Love is a wife having the courage to read a passage of strength at her husband's funeral.

Love is a husband never leaving his wife's side, even when he is no longer alive.

DEATH

"Don't go to Toledo," Erin told me. She and my mom were driving from Columbus, where they had spent the day Christmas shopping. I was heading west from Cleveland, praying that my worst fears were not true. "They aren't life-flighting Dad there anymore."

"Why? What happened? What'd the hospital say? What happened to Dad?" My questions burst out at her as my heart's pace quickened.

"I don't know. I don't know! No one will tell us anything except he's at the hospital in Fremont. We just have to drive to Fremont. I don't know anything else!"

My fingers trembled as I ended the call. I gasped, coughed, and nearly choked. Rapid breaths heaved my chest. A jackhammer thumped inside me, every desperate beat vibrating my body. Tears gushed down my cheeks like rain rushing down a windowpane. My eyes were open, but I saw nothing. I felt the car rumble as it drifted to the edge of the road.

"Let me drive!" my girlfriend screamed. "No!" I shouted as she steadied the wheel. My panic relented. I straightened the car and glanced at the phone in my lap.

An hour earlier, I had learned my father had suffered a heart attack. Now I knew he was dead.

• • •

In many ways, I expected Dad's death. He had even predicted it. "You know, the life expectancy for NFL players is 55. I'll be lucky if I make it that far," he regularly said when asked about the intersection of his health and pro career. Other hints existed besides Dad's words—the recent, uncharacteristic autographs for my sister and niece, the alarming way he had fumbled his words a couple of years ago at a Michigan football game, the increasing forgetfulness Mom patiently combated with reminders and notes.

Dad suffered a stroke in December 2008. Although he recovered, the peach in his face had fled and a glassy glaze had begun to dress his eyes. Then, just months before he died, Dad required a health exam as part of a small workers' compensation lawsuit versus the NFL. Neurologists confirmed that he had suffered a loss of attention and recall from years of football violence. My father, as his death approached, drifted in conversations, his timing imprecise and his words out of context. Dad often seemed lost, as if trapped somewhere inside his faltering brain.

But more than any other reason, I understood the severity of Dad's decline because of the confession he had made to me one evening two years earlier. "Kelly, I'm tired all the time," he had admitted. Though I never expressed my fears to him or anyone else, that night I coped with my tornado of emotions by writing my father's eulogy.

Now I would have to find the courage and composure to speak those words. Could I?

● ● ●

At the hospital, a doctor called Mom, Erin, and me into a separate room away from our family and friends in the waiting area. Dad had dialed 911, the doctor told us. The emergency team found him minutes later in our living room, collapsed atop a smashed end table. He was alive, but barely, and then rushed to the hospital where he suffered a second heart attack. Doctors tried to revive him, but they could do nothing. Dad's life went black. He was 56.

The hospital staff then led us and a few family and friends into a separate room to see Dad. He lay on a bed in the room's center, his forehead bruised and gashed from when he had collapsed. I sat in a chair near the bed, present in the room, but absent, too. I searched for memories of Dad—a laugh I could cling to for comfort or words I could clutch for hope—but nothing appeared. I could see Dad only in *that* moment. He looked helpless but somehow at peace, a wounded man finally able to rest.

We stayed in the room for hours and shared what we knew of Dad's final day. He had spent the morning with Popo. They had eaten lunch together, Popo having a glass of Chardonnay while Dad had a beer. They grinned the big, toothy grin they shared. Stories reached us that several people had seen Dad working in the yard later that afternoon. He shouted jokes as they passed. Mom spoke of the night before when Dad had carried four trips worth of Christmas decorations down three flights of stairs. He had had no pain or shortness of breath, nothing that would foreshadow his end.

One by one, we said our goodbyes. After the room had cleared, I looked into Dad's eyes for the last time, a waterfall cascading from my own. I shook my head between long breaths and long blinks. I touched Dad's cold face with the back of my hand as a parent might check a child for a fever. I kissed his forehead and squeezed his right hand with both of mine.

"I love you, Dad," I said and left the room.

**Erin and Dad during the father and
daughter dance at Erin's wedding, 2005**

A WONDERFUL LIFE

Dad considered himself a failure. The same week that he died, he sat on a couch in our family room next to my mom and questioned what purpose he had served. "Tracy, I'm a waste," he said. "I'm such a failure." [14]

Dad figured he never amounted to much both because of how his football career had ended and because of his lack of fulfillment with life following retirement. His perceived shortcomings burdened him while he never appreciated his positive influence. This was tragic, I think,

---

[14] Dad's favorite movie was *It's a Wonderful Life*. Mom, Dad, Erin, and I watched Frank Capra's tale of morality and consequence that masquerades as a holiday film every Christmas after unwrapping presents. I know Dad identified with the struggle of Jimmy Stewart's character to balance what he had accomplished with the dreams he never attained. I never asked, but I believe my dad hoped for a similar unveiling of purpose as the one Stewart received. Unfortunately, such clarity never arrived.

because Dad mattered in ways observable and unobservable. To spend time with Dad was to spend time with someone who showed each person he met that he or she mattered. His authenticity encouraged others to recognize their own importance. He welcomed and he inspired, but he missed how important this made him.

Dad's memorial service on November 24, 2010, was a must-see event in Fremont. The line to enter the church stretched out the large, ornate front doors and down the sidewalk. The crowd crammed into wooden pews, crouched in aisleways, or stood in the back corners of the balcony to witness the proceedings. I had never seen *any* church this crowded, and I couldn't help but laugh at what Dad might have said at the sight of so many people memorializing him. "Ahh, hell, don't you people have something better to do with your mornings?" I pictured him thinking.

After the service, I spoke with too many people to keep the separate conversations from colliding with each other. I shared memories with his lifelong friends. Others I spoke with had met him once but felt compelled enough by that encounter to pay their tribute. I heard so many kind things about Dad that as morning faded into afternoon, I had to remind people that although my father was a great man, he was no saint.

The truth, as everyone there recognized, was that Dad's life mattered in some way to them. It mattered to his teary-eyed family, to the nephews who idolized him, and to the friends who already missed him. Still, nothing anyone said that day reinforced this more than the final conversation I had before leaving the church.

I'm unsure how many hours I had spent that day discussing my dad's life while standing on the green and white checkered floor of the church's reception area. My feet hurt, and I was hoarse. All I wanted was to retire the paste-on smile I had forced myself to wear all day and drink a cold beer. As I carried a pot of flowers toward the exit sign, I spotted my family's former neighbor, Justin, standing about fifteen yards away near a stand of our family's photos. Justin appeared somber as he observed the collection of memories pinned against a corkboard. Nobody remained in the room except the two of us.

Several years older than me, Justin had lived in an apartment complex next door to my house before his family moved to another part of town when I was in first or second grade. He had an absentee father, and money was always tight. Justin, his mom, and his sister were also little people. I remember that Justin had surgery at Shriners Hospital for Children to straighten his short, bowed legs as much as possible. We had to postpone our backyard football games against each other until after he recovered.

Nearly a decade had passed since I last saw Justin, and I wasn't sure when he last spoke with my dad. Now in his early thirties, he looked older than I remembered. Loose strands of black hair on his cheeks and chin formed the start of a beard. His eyes looked heavy, weighted by the gravity of the moment.

I mustered a weak, half-hearted hello to my old friend. He apologized for missing the service, mentioning something about having to work and reading the start time wrong in the newspaper. I listened with half an ear and thanked him for making it to the reception when he could. My emotions floated somewhere outside my exhausted body.

We made small talk around the softball and football games we played together many years ago and even chuckled at the childhood memory of the wintry afternoon when Dad took us sledding. That day, Justin launched himself off a snowy ramp and into the cold air, smacking his head against the icy ground when he landed.

"I seen some stars," Justin said.

"It looked like it hurt," I offered as consolation.

Justin asked about my mom and sister, and I inquired about his family. He told me how "great" my father was to him, and I thanked him for his words. Silence then separated us—it seemed we had run out of things to say. Slowly, I saw tears form in Justin's eyes before he finally spoke.

"How can life be so unfair that your dad died so young?" Justin asked.

The sincerity in his hurt touched something inside me. My broken heart succumbed to the sadness surrounding it. For five days before this moment, I had insulated myself against the pain ravaging my body. Justin's question shredded my defenses and laid open my wounds. I wept, unable to answer.

Dad had helped Justin in many ways. He brought him to games and sporting events that our family attended, and we included him in all the athletic contests that occurred in and around our house. There were afternoons spent together sledding, at the local fair, or relaxing outside by the pool in my Grandma and Grandpa Lytle's backyard.

I don't know everything Dad did for Justin, but I do remember a time many years after Justin's family moved away when Dad helped him fight a gambling addiction that threatened his ability to work and provide for his family. After graduating high school and starting to work, an obsession with scratch-off lottery tickets had overwhelmed Justin. The addiction consumed him and his paychecks.

Dad spoke and met with Justin often during this time. He checked Justin's spending, monitored his finances, and helped him fight through his crippling habit. I never learned how long the arrangement lasted or even if it worked. All I know is that when Justin needed help, he turned to my dad. And Dad was there to help him, just as he was there to help so many others.

Finding purpose in life is no easy task. To an extent, I think everyone questions where he or she belongs. It seems that too many people underestimate their importance, as I know my dad did. I learned from my father that every person matters and that all of us can inspire others with our words and actions—even something as simple as a hello or well-timed smile. Dad preached this message not by what he said but in how he treated people.

The tenderness in Justin's question said everything about what Dad meant to him, and his tears said everything about what Dad meant to everyone else.

Dad might not have realized it, but he lived a wonderful life.

From Darkness to Light

"What Corrigan wanted was a fully believable God, one you could find in the grime of the everyday. The comfort he got from the hard, cold truth—the filth, the war, the poverty—was that life could be capable of small beauties. He wasn't interested in the glorious tales of the afterlife or the notions of a honey-soaked heaven. To him that was a dressing room for hell. Rather he consoled himself with the fact that, in the real world, when he looked closely into the darkness he might find the presence of a light, damaged and bruised, but a little light all the same."
Colum McCann, *Let the Great World Spin*.

I lost touch with God slowly, over many years, and not from anger or disillusionment, but because I became agnostic about a spiritual presence I no longer felt. God had grown distant, absent from my daily life. The perfect vision of heaven preached to me in church seemed forged, like a neatly packaged version of hope sold for profit in a six-box set. God and I walked different paths because I needed more proof of His or Her existence.

On Christmas Eve 2010, I crammed alongside several members of my family into a tiny nursing home room to visit my mom's father as he recovered from open-heart surgery. Grandpa, 85 years old and still clawing at life, lay in his bed, barely able to smile. We gathered there to wish him a Merry Christmas, except nothing about our situation felt cheerful. Dad had died one month before and my mom, sister, and I were still reeling.

I sat on a metal folding chair in the corner of Grandpa's room with my head down and eyes locked on the floor. My mom, her allergic lungs suffering from the fumes that spewed from the nursing home's newly installed gray carpet, wandered the halls seeking escape. Merry Christmas, Kelly, I thought as I lifted my head and scanned the collection of moping faces scattered among my grandpa's bowling trophies and University of Michigan football memorabilia.

I wanted to know where I could find hope in this scene.

A few minutes later, after my mom had returned to the room, we began our farewells. Then from somewhere in the hallway, I heard the off-key sounds of a Christmas carol. Just outside our room, members of a local church were treating the patients of the nursing home to Christmas songs. A smile overtook my frown. The mood lifted and calm entered my heart for the first time since Dad had died. Despite all the tears I had cried over losing my father, I had survived the first month without him. In this imperfect situation, the carolers had brought me a perfect moment.

When I thankfully read Colum McCann's description of Corrigan in *Let the Great World Spin* a few days later, it occurred to me that I had discovered my God in the midst of sadness and suffering while sitting in a stuffy nursing home. Until that point, my recent life had felt too removed from religion to hear the answers I sought from the cryptic God that I peppered with questions about morality. Like Corrigan, I needed a God willing to roll up His or Her sleeves and shine some light into the sadness churning my insides. I didn't need God's promise that one day I would greet my father in a majestic, perfect reunion in heaven. Instead, I needed God to help me remember how to smile through the day-to-day. I needed hope.

MORE

Dad's death compelled me to believe I needed to change history. In the months after he died, I wanted something better from our relationship. I call it the curse of more, and it threatened to ruin my memories of my father.

I first felt something was wrong five months after Dad died. On April 30, 2011, the Sandusky County Board of Developmental Disabilities (SCBDD) dedicated its learning and activity center to Dad for his efforts with the organization. The SCBDD provides individuals with developmental disabilities and their families with services and support to enhance the quality of their everyday lives. Dad served the SCBDD as a board member and active volunteer during his final years.

Speakers that afternoon remembered Dad for his sense of humor, caring, and selflessness. He had been instrumental in finding and securing financing for the new center. For this, the crowd demonstrated deep gratitude. The spirit of the dedication floored me. I left that day prouder of Dad for his efforts with the SCBDD than for anything he had ever accomplished as an athlete. But I resented him, too, because the program revealed to me aspects of my dad I had missed out on.

As time passed, I kept reflecting on the dedication. I found myself unable to celebrate the moment. Instead, I became annoyed at how little I understood about why Dad cared so much for helping the individuals at this particular center. Dad and I had spoken many times of his involvement with the SCBDD, but he shielded any window into feelings with his matter-of-factness. "Just trying to help," he would say, and I would let the moment pass.

Dad skirted the "why" behind his motivations with the SCBDD just as he never spoke about all the work he did for organizations like the March of Dimes and Special Olympics during and after his Bronco days. I remember him paying a running tab at a local diner so a homeless man he knew could eat breakfast. He never mentioned why, just as he never spoke about other acts of kindness.

"What's reason got to do with anything?" I picture him responding to my imagined pleas for understanding. "It's the right thing to do. What else do I need to explain?"

In life, I accepted the wall Dad constructed. In death, I wanted revelations of what made him tick. The whisper intensified. I wanted more.

Frustration spread like an infection in the months that followed the SCBDD dedication. I obsessed over many of our conversations. Even as I wrote the stories of appreciation within this book, I saw where our bond had failed instead of succeeded. I saw athletics, a cornerstone of our interactions, as a hindrance rather than a facilitator. For the first time, I challenged the sanctity of our reliance on sports as an intimate bond.

Communicating with much emotional weight never came easy to Dad, and it isn't easy for me. Maybe the playing fields, where actions and quiet sacrifice speak louder than words, were the culprit. Sports gave our relationship an outlet, a platform for discussing hopes through the lens of an upcoming football game or exposing regret for lost opportunities under the guise of missed free throws at the end of a youth basketball tournament.

I felt comfortable speaking to Dad about my fears of failure as long as I revealed those fears during a talk about nerves before a track meet. Dad could empathize. "Sometimes I was scared to play before a big game," he would tell me. "I was that nervous. But I knew the more nervous I was, the better I would play."

Dad and I relied on sports for purpose. We anchored our conversations in athletics because doing so meant we never had to admit how directionless we would have felt without its regimens and clear goals. Vulnerability could exist as long as it occurred between the white lines of a football field.

We discussed more than sports, of course, but when I was growing up I always found it easier to discuss practices and game preparation instead of topics with more substance. We analyzed opponents and considered past performances as the means to improve future ones. Although we chatted about schoolwork, college, and girls, and we made veiled references to the future, nothing carried the same significance as talking sports. The more I grieved over Dad's death, the emptier I perceived what we had shared. In a relationship strong enough to accept any conversation, why didn't we talk about more?

The worst part, I believe, is that neither Dad nor I wanted or believed in such constrained exchanges. We simply didn't know anything different. Sports gave our relationship a default setting that we accepted as enough. Despite all the talking we did, I came to wonder what I had missed. Mixed with all the appreciation I felt for my father was a feeling that he hadn't cut it. I let hindsight, with its promise for perfection, strip from me the specialness of the past. These emotions hurt.

Then, things changed. Maybe I wrote myself through the curse or enough time passed for my feelings to shift. Maybe I overcame my selfishness, or I finally appreciated that life, despite its flaws, is precious.

I'm not sure what happened. I still have questions, and this book is full of lost opportunities that weigh on me and always will. But what time has taught is how lucky I am to have enjoyed what I did with my dad.

I can now let my mind return without regret to the afternoon when the SCBDD dedicated its activity center. No, Dad and I never discussed his motivations for helping. And yes, at times we let the familiarity and comfort of sports replace the possibility for more emotional interactions. So what? The memories I do have are what matter.

Dad valued others, and I never pressed him about why. I didn't need to, though, because I saw it firsthand in a rescue of two strangers out of gas and out of luck, stuck on the side of the road on a winter night. And I watched young kids from all backgrounds, some blessed by fate and some cursed by it, leave the neighborhood softball games Dad hosted believing more in their own special importance after having been included in hours of play. Sports helped me appreciate perseverance and self-sacrifice. The talks I shared with Dad reinforced these traits. I learned through such moments. Call that cliché. I call it influential.

I would give anything for more time with Dad. But it occurs to me, at the end of this journey, that a point of my grief was to understand how to celebrate everything I had while relinquishing the burden of wanting more from the person I lost.

Dad and I four months before he died, 2010

The Final Letter

Dear Dad,

I've wanted to write a book since I was a kid. Now, I've done it. I wrote a book, and I wrote it about us. Now the question is, how do I end it? How do I place the final period on the final word of the final sentence of this collection of thanks?

The truth is that I'm scared to finish writing because I'm scared to say goodbye. This book brought me closer to you, and after over two years of writing, I don't want to let go. Closing the final chapter scares me. I don't know what happens to us next.

Dad, the enormity of loss suffocated me when you died. I needed an outlet for my pain. I *needed* to write this book. Writing let me heal. Writing filled the void of losing my best friend. Even though you were gone, the writing kept us close. Now, the writing is finished.

I started this book by scribbling a letter to you a year after you died. That day, I fought tears and wrote onto sheets of yellow paper marked by coffee stains and margin notes of rambling reflection. Frustration over missed opportunities quickened my every heartbeat. Remorse over my loss shortened each breath. I thanked you for being my friend and condemned you for being unhappy with life after football. I praised the way you taught me to value others above myself and admonished you for the way your dissatisfaction cultivated restlessness in me.

Putting my feelings into words hurt, but I endured.

That first letter spawned a series of them. Heartbreak, my fear of failure, regrets for my life and yours, the guilt I carried for celebrating your painkiller addiction, and hopes I had never appreciated poured from me. I relinquished my ego and accepted the catharsis of honest vulnerability. When I exhaled after months of writing, I realized I had created a hodgepodge of personal revelations, father and son lessons, questions that we left unasked and unanswered, and the emotional foundation for this book.

Dad, I wrote these stories to relive our experiences, to remember what it felt like to sit at your old bar on Monday nights, watching football on a small television hanging from the wall and listening to grown-ups talk sports and life. I wanted to be a kid playing catch with my dad. I wanted another chance at conversations that time has given me the courage to have with you.

Mostly, I wrote to say thank you. Thank you for what you meant to Mom, Erin, and me. Thank you for teaching me compassion, humility, the value of family, and for showing me how to believe in myself.

The right closing, if any exists, escapes me. Saying goodbye is never easy, so I'll say it the way we did many times over many years: Goodbye my friend. I'll see you when I see you.

Love,
Kelly

ACKNOWLEDGMENTS

Writing a book is hard work. Thanking everyone who made it possible is even harder.

To my mom and my sister Erin, thank you. Mom, you are the strength of our family and a constant source of guidance for Erin and me. This book might reflect the lessons I learned from Dad that shape me, but the most important lessons in compassion and caring I learned from you.

Erin, I can already see your tears as you read these memories of our dad. You are caring, generous, and strong-willed. You mean the world to me.

To my aunts, uncles, and cousins, I apologize for subjecting you to the terrifying early versions of this book, and I thank you for your constructive insights and memories of my father.

I owe a special thank you to George Wenger. Uncle George, you received the roughest of drafts, and your initial support gave me the courage to continue writing.

Thank you to the eloquent Tom Hadley for sharing your hilarious and sometimes obscene tales of your friendship with my dad. Though I borrowed some of your words for this book, my stories cannot do yours justice.

T. L. Champion, thank you for encouraging me to write the original letter that eventually inspired this book. You believed in these stories from the beginning and urged me to write with emotional fearlessness. In doing so, you helped me grow as a person and as a writer.

Thank you to Norm Friedman for agreeing to carry me (and this book) across the finish line. Your editing, eye for detail, suggestions, and efforts to restrain my wordiness improved each chapter. I still have nightmares about the red ink spilled on each chapter.

Thank you to Stacie King for letting me laugh, cry, pound the wall in frustration, and heal as I wrote many of these stories. Most importantly, thank you for never allowing me to question why I had to keep writing when the toll of my emotions made me consider stopping.

Thank you to every friend who provided feedback on the initial drafts, especially Ross Reineck, Bryan Root, Mike Weishuhn, Solomon Barnett, and Drew Geant. Your advice brought direction and clarity to this book.

One conversation can change our lives forever. Thank you, Andy Breiner, for sharing your story with me at Keens Steakhouse in Manhattan. Your honesty inspired me, and I will never forget your words.

Finally, I want to thank my dad, whose lessons, humor, and spirit fill these pages.

Made in the USA
Las Vegas, NV
11 February 2023